*A Bio-Bibliography of*
*Countée P. Cullen*
*1903-1946*

## Contributions in Afro-American and African Studies

# A Bio-Bibliography of Countée P. Cullen 1903-1946

MARGARET PERRY

Foreword by Don M. Wolfe

Contributions in Afro-American
and African Studies, Number 8

A Negro Universities Press Publication

Greenwood Publishing Corporation
Westport, Connecticut

Copyright © 1971 by *Margaret Perry*

Lines from "To Lovers of Earth: Fair Warning" and "Uncle Jim" are from *Copper Sun*, by Countée Cullen, copyright 1927 by Harper & Brothers; renewed 1955 by Ida M. Cullen. Reprinted with permission.

Lines from "Pity the Deep in Love," "Incident," "Sonnet," "Heritage," "Wisdom Cometh with the Years," "A Song of Praise," "Saturday's Child," "For Paul Lawrence Dunbar," "For a Lady I Know," "For a Mouthy Woman," *The Black Christ*, "Red," "Variations on a Theme," "The Wise," "Death to the Poor," *The Ballad of the Brown Girl*, "To John Keats, Poet. At Springtime," and "The Shroud of Color" are from *On These I Stand*, by Countée Cullen, copyright 1947 by Harper & Row, Publishers, Incorporated. Reprinted with permission.

Lines from "Renascence" and "God's World" are from *Collected Poems*, by Edna St. Vincent Millay, copyright 1959 by Harper & Row, Publishers, Incorporated. Reprinted with permission.

Library of Congress Catalog Card Number: 75-105995
SBN: 8371-3325-4

A Negro Universities Press Publication
Greenwood Publishing Corporation
51 Riverside Avenue, Westport, Connecticut 06880

Printed in the United States of America

*To My Mother*

# Contents

# CONTENTS

# Foreword

In bringing together this body of materials about
Countée Cullen, Margaret Perry has performed a valuable
service to the illumination of American literature. Her
notes on Cullen's life, taken in good part from unpublished
correspondence, are in themselves invaluable and timely.
Miss Perry's own critical comments on key passages from
the various collections of Cullen's poetry provide a survey
of vital judgments no scholar of American poetry will wish
to pass by. If they are more derivative than original, they
trace in substance the rich mosaic of Cullen's art. Miss
Perry's comparisons of Cullen's art with that of Robinson,
Millay, and Cullen's idol, Keats, are rich and evocative, as
is the contrast between Cullen and Langston Hughes.
Finally, the bibliography of Cullen's works and the reviews
of his books, brought together with patient thoroughness
and loving care, are invaluable to future scholars for their
comprehensiveness alone.

Miss Perry's critical comments, her very selection from Cullen's lines and stanzas, lead us back with amazement and delight to a structured, orderly intellectual world, a world described in rhymes reminiscent of Keats, but full of images and ideas only one poet, unique in psyche and outlook, could bring to birth. Consider, for example, the first poem in *On These I Stand*, Cullen's last book, and a collection of poems the poet thought to be his best work. It was published after his death in 1946 at the age of forty-three:

YET DO I MARVEL

I doubt not God is good, well-meaning, kind,
And did He stoop to quibble could tell why
The little buried mole continues blind,
Why flesh that mirrors Him must some day die,
Make plain the reason tortured Tantalus
Is baited by the fickle fruit, declare
If merely brute caprice dooms Sisyphus
To struggle up a never-ending stair.
Inscrutable His ways are, and immune
To catechism by a mind too strewn
With petty cares to slightly understand
What awful brain compels His awful hand
Yet do I marvel at this curious thing:
To make a poet black, and bid him sing!

In these lines we may trace a mind still deeply involved in the mysteries of ultimate rationality and the religious needs of his childhood; the poet gropes and struggles for the assurance of his childhood in the midst of oppressive realities, the chief of which is: "To make a poet black, and bid him sing!" This is a line no other poet on the American scene could have written. Would any other American poet have struck off the image of the mole: a necessary contrast to the weak abstractions of the first line?

I like the passage Miss Perry quotes from Arna Bontemps: "Cullen was in many ways an old-fashioned poet. He never ventured very far from the Methodist parsonage in which he grew up in New York. A foster child, drawn into this shelter at an early age, he continued to cherish it gratefully. He gave his adopted parents a devotion, one is almost inclined to say a submission, only rarely rendered by natural sons. But it was all a part of his own choice. He did not stand in fear of his foster parents." Owen Dodson's characterization of Cullen spoke also for the poet's family and friends: "He was faithful, loyal, quiet, tender." In quoting such passages, Miss Perry traces the sturdy uprightness and idealism of Cullen's childhood, traits that sustained and deepened his creative aspirations.

In his poem, "Fruit of the Flower," Cullen portrays his parents with touches of loving irony. First we see the father:

> My father is a quiet man
> With sober, steady ways;
> For simile, a folded fan;
> His nights are like his days.

Cullen's poems are seldom without a magical phrase or two, such as the folded fan image in this stanza. Then the mother:

> Why should she think it devil's art
> That all my songs should be
> Of love and lovers, broken heart,
> And wild sweet agony?

Beneath the sedateness of his parents Cullen sensed their own youth of long ago. He could see his father's eyes "boast how full his life had been." In those eyes there would flash now and then "the languid ghost of some still sacred sin." Though Cullen's mother "sings chants of God," he has seen "a bit of checkered sod set all her flesh aquiver." In Cullen's heart, as all who knew him testify, there was no room for sudden hate even of white people; least of all did his heart burn suddenly with a blaze of hatred for his parents or their friends. Indeed he felt that they entered into his youthful feelings and yearnings as easily as he into their less turbulent ones.

Milton called rhyme "a trivial thing, of no true musical delight." Much as I love Milton (and much as I believe that accent on rhyme is destructive in early attempts to write poetry), I do not find rhymes objectionable in the poetry of Countée Cullen. Indeed the harsh dilemmas of American life take on sharper focus in his rhymed stanzas than I have found in those poets of rebellion who believe that the disregard of poetic tradition is equivalent to excellence. Consider, for example, these lines from Cullen's poem, "Incident":

> Once riding in old Baltimore,
>   Heart-filled, head-filled with glee,
> I saw a Baltimorean
>   Kept looking straight at me.
>
> Now I was eight and very small,
>   And he was no whit bigger,
> And so I smiled, but he poked out
>   His tongue, and called me, "Nigger."

# FOREWORD

I saw the whole of Baltimore
From May until December;
Of all the things that happened there
That's all that I remember.

This poem, though deficient in electric imagery, has drama intensified by the very restraint of its rhymes. In an instant we are brought to the spot: a black boy riding about in Baltimore; it is spring, and his heart is full of joy and trust, expecting only love on such a benign day. Then suddenly a thunderbolt in the child's world—to reverberate in all the years to come. Thus Cullen's appeal to conscience: a far greater power in American life than violence and hatred. In this unforgettable drama of one moment in a little boy's life, reaching deep into the experience of Americans young and old, the orderly rhymes intensify the bruising shock to the little boy's spirit.

Lovers of American literature are indebted to Margaret Perry for her careful preliminary study of Cullen's contributions to American literature. Had it not been for her work, many lovers of poetry would not have explored some of the deep recesses of Cullen's art and the reach of his aspirations. When Cullen wrote, "I have my own soul's ecstasy," he expressed his need to "leave something so written to aftertimes as they should not willingly let it die."

DON M. WOLFE

# Preface

The work of a good poet never dies with the man, but the seemingly commonplace chore of recording the location of his individual works—either in their original sources or in anthologies—and of noting significant articles concerning the man, is a service infrequently performed for our modern poets. This is especially true for the black poet. It is hoped that this book will renew interest in the life and work of Countée P. Cullen, a Negro poet who retained the attention of leading critics throughout his career.

Mr. Cullen, one of a group of younger poets, began the most fruitful part of his career in the 1920s, during the period known as "The Harlem Renaissance," noted for a flowering of talent among Negro artists. As Cullen wrote: "Never before has such an acute interest existed in the Negro as a possible artist. Literary, musical and theatrical doors are opening for him at the touch of the knob."[*]

[*] Countée Cullen, "The Negro Sings his Soul," *Survey Graphic* 7 (September 1925):583.

Yet, Mr. Cullen was not considered only as a poet; he was a scholar and a man committed to helping his race achieve greater significance in American life. The brief biographical sketch and the discussion of Mr. Cullen's poetry preceding the bibliography, will enable the reader to understand more clearly this poet's place in modern American literature.

The primary purpose of this book is to provide a practical guide for those searching for a particular poem by Mr. Cullen. Bibliographical information about his other works, especially some of his more obscure writings, is included in order to make this work as comprehensive as possible. It is the wish of the writer to stimulate the reader's interest in both the man and the man-as-writer.

The scope, then, is broad. Certain geographical restrictions, however, have limited the comprehensiveness of this work. The author was unable to visit personally all of the known holdings of Cullen material. Knowledge of these collections had to be gained through correspondence, and necessarily resulted in certain bibliographic difficulties, most of which have been resolved. After the completion of the manuscript, but too late for inclusion in the book, two collections were brought to the author's attention: unspecified holdings at the Harvard University Library, and a small collection of Cullen memorabilia owned by Mr. Glenn Carrington of New York City. One anticipates the opportunity to produce a second, revised and expanded, edition of this bibliography at some appropriate time in the future.

# *Acknowledgments*

Grateful acknowledgment is made to the following for giving their kind permission to reprint from works in their possession.

The Catholic University of America, Department of Librarianship, gave permission to Margaret Perry to publish her thesis, "A Bio-Bibliography of Countée P. Cullen, 1903–1946," (1959).

Letters quoted in Chapter 1 are printed by the kind permission of Yale University Library and Mrs. Ida M. Cullen: Cullen to Harold Jackman, 1 July 1923; Cullen to Jackman, 25 August 1923; Cullen to Carl Van Vechten, 29 April 1926; Cullen to Jackman, 10 August 1923; Cullen to Jackman, 18 August 1923; Cullen to Jackman, 7 April 1926; Cullen to Jackman, 28 July 1926; Cullen to Witter Bynner, 22 November 1929; Cullen to Edward Atkinson, 1 August 1937; Cullen to Atkinson, 15 August 1937; and Cullen to Atkinson, 2 August 1938. Also quoted in Chapter 1 are Cullen's "French Notebook" and a manuscript synopsis of *One Way to Heaven*.

Harper & Row gave permission to reprint lines from "To Lovers of Earth: Fair Warning" and "Uncle Jim" from *Copper Sun* by Countée Cullen; "Pity the Deep in Love," "Incident," "Sonnet," "Heritage," "Wisdom Cometh with the Years," "A Song of Praise," "Saturday's Child," "For Paul Lawrence Dunbar," "For a Lady I Know," "For a Mouthy Woman," *The Black Christ*, "Red," "Variations on a Theme," "The Wise," "Death to the Poor," *The Ballad of the Brown Girl*, "To John Keats, Poet At Springtime," and "The Shroud of Color" from *On These I Stand* by Countée Cullen; and "Renascence" and "God's World" from *Collected Poems* by Edna St. Vincent Millay. Lines from "Renascence" and "God's World" are also printed by permission of Mrs. Norma Millay Ellis.

Mrs. Van Vechten gave her kind permission to use the photograph taken by Carl Van Vechten as the frontispiece.

Acknowledgment must be given to Dom Bernard Theall, O.S.B., of the Catholic University of America, who suggested Cullen as a subject for study. The author also wishes to acknowledge the very friendly and gracious help given her by Mrs. Ida Mae Cullen, the widow of the poet. It was she who made available the unpublished works of Countée Cullen, many clippings kept by the poet, and letters to him from Witter Bynner and E. A. Robinson.

Other persons who must be mentioned for the help they gave to the author are Mrs. Jean B. Hutson, Curator of the Schomburg Collection (New York Public Library); the late Harold Jackman; Miss Ivie Jackman; Mr. Owen Dodson; Mr. William Fuller Brown, Jr.; Mrs. Beulah Reimherr; Mrs. Rose Tresser of De Witt-Clinton High School;

the librarians at Howard and Fisk universities, Mr. Louis Pedulla, Mr. John Creecy, and Miss Cosette Stern. Special thanks must also be given to the staff at the Beinecke Rare Books Library at Yale University (especially Mrs. Anne Whelpley), and to the following former classmates of Countée Cullen: Mr. Paul Titus, Mr. Milton M. Bergerman, Mr. Irving Kahn, Mr. Sidney Jarcho, and Mr. Louis Orgel.

The interest and enthusiasm of all of these people helped the writer to realize the importance of acquainting the reading public with Mr. Cullen and his work. It is hoped that the present book will perform this for one writer, too often overlooked, who enriched the literature of his native land.

## PART I

# The Man and His Poetry

# 1

## The Life of
## Cullen

THE child was born Countée Porter;
the boy and man became Countée P. Cullen. Even before
his first book of poetry was published in 1925, Countée
Cullen was a known and admired figure in the literary
world. Although it is impossible here to present a definitive
biography of this poet, some mention of his life, his character, his writings, and his place in American literature is
necessary to make this bibliography a more meaningful tool.

Countée P. Cullen was born in New York City on
30 May 1903. He lived with his grandmother until her
death in 1918. This period of Cullen's life is too undocu-
mented to be sure of how he lived and of what he did. One
must speculate that he was a good reader and a more than
average student, for he wrote his first published poem in
free verse at the age of fourteen.[1] In 1918 he was adopted
by the Reverend and Mrs. Frederick A. Cullen. Reverend
Cullen was founder and minister of the Salem Methodist

Episcopal Church in New York City. It is interesting to note in Rev. Cullen's own autobiography that he never mentions his son's birth or adoption. Countée simply appears from time to time in this brief book as "my son Countée Cullen."[2]

Cullen received his early education in the New York public schools and distinguished himself when he was a student at DeWitt-Clinton High School. This high school has had many graduates in all professional fields, but even a partial listing would serve to indicate the calibre of literary artists it has produced: Lionel Trilling, Sidney Skolsky, Nicholas Samstag, Emil Capouya, and James Baldwin, for example. It would not be an exaggeration to say that Cullen flourished like a blossoming flower while attending high school. He was a member of the Inter-High School Poetry Society and won second prize for a poem, "In Memory of Lincoln," in a contest conducted by the Sorosis Club at DeWitt-Clinton. He won first place in a Douglas Fairbanks oratorical contest for his speech "God and the Negro." The second-prize winner, Mr. Milton M. Bergerman, has remarked recently: "My subject was 'The Functions of Government.' . . . The audience was spellbound [listening to Cullen] and I was amazed to get such terrific opposition. Is there any wonder that he won!"[3]

Other distinctions Cullen achieved were the editorship of the *Clinton News*, the high school weekly, the vice-presidency of his senior class, and the leadership of Arista— the highest scholastic honor given at his high school.[4]

In his senior year Cullen was the editor of the senior edition of the school literary magazine, *The Magpie*. Many of his poems first appeared in this distinctive high school journal. It was here he wrote: "Poet, poet what's your

mission/Here mid earth's grief and pain? . . . Poet, poet
what do you ask/As pay for each glad song?/Thy thanks
will pay me doubly well/And last my whole life long."[5]
In January 1921 his ever-famous "I Have a Rendezvous with
Life" was printed in the magazine. This poem, inspired
by Seeger's famous antithetical verses, brought Cullen
public recognition; he was awarded a prize for it in a
contest sponsored by the Federation of Women's Clubs.

Countée Cullen was one of very few Negroes at
DeWitt-Clinton High School. As shown by the number of
activities in which he was a leader, Cullen had few difficulties because of his race. He was intelligent and sensitive—
and these traits, recognized and respected, were certainly
his passkey to acceptance into the world in which he was
living. A former classmate, Cullen's junior by one or two
years, reminisced recently: "He was a very energetic extro-
vert with a fairly high academic standing. I suspect that
he was a year or two older than we were, at least he gave
the impression that he was a worldly man while we were
still acting like high school kids."[6] Therefore, on Thursday
evening, 26 January 1922, when friends and parents gathered
for the graduation exercises, it was not surprising to find
Cullen's name scattered throughout the "Special Honors"
section of the Commencement Exercises program. He received honors in Latin, Mathematics, History, English,
French, and General Honors; it was a distinguished end to
his childhood. He was soon to start his college career at
New York University.

In 1923 he won the second prize in the Witter Bynner
undergraduate poetry contest, sponsored by the Poetry
Society of America. The poem that won this prize was
"The Ballad of the Brown Girl." At the time he won this

honor Cullen said he was interested in poetry for poetry's sake and not for propaganda purposes. "In spite of myself, however," he added, "I find that I am actuated by a strong sense of race consciousness. This grows upon me, I find, as I grow older; and although I struggle against it, it colors my writing, I fear, in spite of everything I can do. There have been many things in my life that have hurt me, and I find that the surest relief from these hurts is in writing."[7] He won the second prize again in 1924; and in 1925 he won the first prize.

To help his family with the finances of his education, Cullen worked as a bus boy at the Traymore Hotel in Atlantic City during the summers. In July 1923 he wrote to his lifelong friend, Harold Jackman: "It is by no means a position, just a job, but it gives me time to study some of the vermin of the race, and since three-fourths of every race is vermin, I am in with the masses. Donald [Duff] would love this atmosphere, but my bourgois [sic] soul receives it as one takes an emetic—with disgust. The place has inspired two poems. For that the vermin be praised! You see I am not at all a democratic person. I believe in an aristocracy of the soul."[8] He was to feel this all of his life; yet this did not imply any desire to escape his racial surroundings or his racial feelings. During that same summer he wrote Jackman again on the effects of listening to a jazz group at a party he attended: "It got into my blood and coursed through every vein making me giddy. I lived more poetry last night than I ever wrote. . . . Cher ami, you have not lived unless you have felt as I did; I was wild, primeval, uncivilized (although I danced decorously)—and careless of it all."[9] This conflict of his nature—cool, intellectual, warm, passionate—would reveal itself in his poetry throughout his life.

An important year in the life of Countée Cullen was 1925. In March he was one of eleven elected to Phi Beta Kappa at New York University. In the May issue of *Opportunity: Journal of Negro Life*, there was an announcement of Cullen's receipt of second prize in its literary contest. Langston Hughes won first prize for his "The Weary Blues;" Cullen's prize-winning poem was "To One Who Said Me Nay." There was at least one critic, Eugene Gordon, who felt Cullen should have received the first prize. Gordon, in a newspaper letter, labeled Hughes's poem "a silly jingle."[10] But Clement Wood defended the choice[11]—and Cullen, always fair-minded and generous, did not lower his dignity to comment at all on this minor controversy. Cullen also won the John Reed Memorial Prize, awarded by *Poetry* magazine, for his poem "Threnody for a Brown Girl."

Since 1923, his poetry had been appearing in various nationwide journals: *The Bookman, Opportunity, Crisis* (the official magazine of the National Association for the Advancement of Colored People), *Poetry* and *Harper's*. Thus, by 1925, Cullen was able to have his first book appear—*Color,* published by Harper & Brothers. Cullen was at Harvard by this time, working towards a master's degree in English.

In a letter to Carl Van Vechten, Cullen wrote: "I am hoping the book will make at least a slight stir, which will help me get some readings to do while up here. . . . You see, I'd like to contribute something toward my expenses while here."[12] The book did receive a great deal of notice from the literary world, and many critics were warm and sympathetic in their praise of the collection. George M. Dillon, in his review in *Poetry*, wrote: "This first volume of musical verse offers promise for its author, shows him to be a young poet of uncommon earnestness and diligence. Serious purpose and careful work are apparent in all of his poems. One feels that he will cultivate his fine talent with intelligence, and reap its full harvest."[13]

In the *Crisis* contest of 1926, Cullen won the second prize for "Thoughts in a Zoo." He also sustained an insulting experience that reveals how free he was of animosity, even when he was a victim of hatred and injustice. In the spring of 1926 he was invited to speak to the Baltimore City Club at the Hotel Emerson. In a letter to Carl Van Vechten he explained that "on learning that I was a Negro the hotel management would not permit the club to have me there, nor could the club secure another hotel or even a theatre in Baltimore where a Negro poet might read to them. As yet I have not written my second diatribe against Baltimore. Anyhow what good would it do?"[14]

During this same year he was appointed assistant editor of *Opportunity*—a position he held until 1928. This was the period during which he wrote his editorials and short book reviews for the feature called "The Dark Tower." He received the Harmon Foundation's award in literature at a ceremony held at St. Mark's Church in New York City in January 1927.

*Copper Sun*, the second book of Countée Cullen's collected poems, was published by Harper in 1927. The reviews of this book ranged from E. Merrill Root's panegyrical approbation in *Opportunity*[15] to Emanuel Eisenberg's unequivocal rejection in *The Bookman*.[16] The general opinion was that, even though many of the poems in this collection measured up to those in the first book, Cullen had not yet matured in his themes or in his expression. The publication of this second book, however, was preceded by a grant by the Guggenheim Fund for a year's study abroad, where he was planning to give full time to his writing.[17]

Prior to his departure for France, Cullen and Nina Yolande DuBois, the daughter of W. E. B. DuBois (editor of *Crisis*, writer, scholar, and teacher), were married on 10 April 1928 in his father's church.[18] It was a storybook alliance—popular young poet, son of a solid and successful minister, and much-sought, well-bred daughter of one of the most famous Negroes in the world—but it was not a hasty decision. Countée and Yolande had known one another since the summer of 1923. At that time he wrote to Harold Jackman: "I have just returned from paying my first call on Yolande DuBois who is stopping a stone's throw away from my house. She pleases me without any reservations. No, she is not beautiful but one is drawn to her by some indefinable magnetism of refinement and soulful honesty. I am glad that you were helpful in making it possible for me to form her acquaintance. . . . Tell me how you maneuvered [*sic*] in order to take Miss DuBois out. I would like to play the gallant cavalier in order to talk to her alone, so as to verify my first impressions of her. . . . Perhaps when you get down [to Pleasantville, N. J., where the Cullens had a summer home] I may make some progress under your tutelage. Where did you learn?"[19]

But Cullen was a loyal friend even though, smitten as he was with young Miss DuBois, it must have been a difficult stance. In another letter to Jackman eight days later he wrote: "Yolande DuBois and I were out driving Thursday evening and I had an opportunity to study her at close range. My delight in her increased fourfold. What she lacks in beauty is compensated for her by her naive

9

frankness. Candor can always enthrall me. . . . Will it be a match between you two, I wonder? . . . The lady holds you in an esteem which the most high gods would envy. . . . Later, as even the cognoscenti sometimes do, we talked platitudes about youth and love, and I suppose I was somewhat gallant, but, never fear; the way lies open to you."[20]

The autumnal season was a reminder to both young people that they had to finish their education, he at New York University, she at Fisk. Besides, Cullen was to experience the throes of love many times before he made the final choice of Yolande. It is almost amusing to note how typically young-gallant-about-town was his dilemma when he was doing his graduate work at Harvard. He wrote to Jackman: "Being somewhat in your own predicament, I am interested in your confession that you are in love, temporarily speaking. . . . I fear my trials are harder than yours, for my passion is not concentrated, but divided between Miss Sydonia Byrd and Miss Fiona Braithwaite. . . . Rumor has already engaged me to both the young ladies who share my unstable affections; so that for the first time in my life I feel what it means to be a shiek [*sic*]—even if only on a small scale."[21] No matter how he thought he was suffering, at least he had a sense of humor! These wavering feelings of affection for three girls must have been relieved by the trip he made to Europe and the Holy Land with his father. Countée was able to practice his French and visit the places he had merely known about through books (of the Nile and Jordan rivers he wrote: "It is interesting to note what poignant associations these streams have to him [his father] as a minister, while to me they are two muddy colored rivers.").[22] Marriage was a matter for the future.

Two and a half months after his marriage, Cullen left

for France in the company of his foster father and of his friend Harold Jackman. The young Mrs. Cullen joined her husband later.[23] The marriage, seemingly made up of all of the right ingredients, lasted only for a year. No one has stated specifically why the marriage failed. There may be a clue in one of the exercises Cullen wrote in his "French Notebook." This contains notes for his classes, his translations of his own poems, and compositions he was assigned to write: There was a concert at the Salle Pleyel; listening to the music of Beethoven, he nearly cries. He asks himself if he is in love. If so, with whom and why? Then he writes: "For a long time I've had enough of love, enough of marriage. If I am wise, I won't take that up again." (The original phrase, changed by Cullen or perhaps his teacher, states "I won't fall for a second time into the same hole.") He goes on to write that he won't be taken in by "brilliant grey eyes, a little too bright, by a well-rounded shape, but supporting a head stuffed with straw."[24] It was a harsh judgment, if this composition actually reflects his feelings at that time. In any case, a divorce was granted to Mrs. Cullen in Paris, in March of 1930.

During his stay abroad, Countée Cullen wrote a series of articles that appeared in *Crisis* in the spring and summer of 1929. Mr. Arna Bontemps, a friend and collaborator of Mr. Cullen, analyzed this period of Countée Cullen's life and came to the conclusion that the poet was hoping for a resurgence of his creative powers. As Mr. Bontemps expressed it:

> His stay in France was extended a year beyond his original plans, but that wasn't enough. His spring-time leaves had fallen, and he was still waiting for a

new season to bring another yield. He kept writing
as a matter of habit, and the little shelf of his books
increased steadily, but that wasn't the real thing;
that wasn't what he was waiting for. A decade later
he wrote a friend: "My muse is either dead or tak-
ing a twenty-year sleep."[25]

Despite Countée Cullen's own concern over his poetry,
despite occasional comments from reviewers about his lack
of growth as a poet during the few years that his work had
been published (he was not yet thirty), his third book, *The
Black Christ*, published in 1929, was received with more
approval than his second. (His friend Witter Bynner, however, did not like it and asked him to "snap out of it, dear
fellow. . . . Don't let yourself be crucified on a Guggenheim
cross, if that's what it is.")[26]

The next work to be published was Cullen's only novel,
*One Way to Heaven* (1932). It is a story of Harlem, of
two strata of life in this unique area. In a synopsis, written by the author, one learns that:

The novel is a two-toned picture. High life among
the high lights of Harlem, the decadent intelligent-
zia [*sic*], mad, witty, laughable, pretentious, white
negro lovers [*sic*] who rage at discrimination, light
brown negresses who laugh at it and shiny blacks
who ape the white four hundred. Another note
beats through the lives of Mattie and Sam and aunt
[*sic*] Mathilda and the negro preacher, who expresses
direct emotions of a simple people; their vices and
virtues, who love and hate and laugh and suffer and
enjoy, who believe with ferver [*sic*] and live with
faith. Into the fierce reality of their lives comes the

empty echo of Constantia Brandon's dry laughter at the absurdities she creates and the society she made.[27]

In 1932 "Cullen, to the surprise of many, announced that he was joining the Foster and Ford Committee, a group of prominent writers . . . pledged to support the Communist ticket in the 1932 elections."[28] Although this was completely true, Cullen made this commitment solely on the belief that the Communist party was the only one interested in the poor and dispossessed. Mr. Cullen was never an active member of the party and his support of it cannot be considered a serious blot on his career.

There were two more books of his collected poetry published in Mr. Cullen's lifetime: *The Medea, and Some Poems* (1935) and *The Lost Zoo*, which appeared in 1940. The first book was a modern rendition of the *Medea* of Euripides, written for Rose McClendon, star of *In Abraham's Bosom*. This adaptation was written in prose, except the choruses which were in verse and were set to music by Virgil Thomson for the stage version. *The Lost Zoo* was Cullen's reproof to those who had accused him of having no humor, for these poems—"for the young, but not too young"—show a lightness of spirit and a keen sense of humor in this essentially lyric poet.

Countée Cullen found unlimited freedom in France, as did many of the Negro artists of the 1920s and 1930s; but he contented himself with several summer visits after he returned to the United States in 1930. (While there he had spent much time in the company of the Negro sculptress Augusta Savage who was a friend to scores of Americans— Negro and white, artist and nonartist.) His "French Note-

book" reveals his competence in the language, and his letters to friends reveal his love for the country. Writing to
his good friend Edward Atkinson from Paris in 1937, he
declared: "These are really what we may call halcyon days.
And yet so ungrateful is the heart of man, that I am not
completely satisfied."[29] Europe in the summer of 1937 was
in a mood far different from the gay ambiance surrounding
Countée when he made his first trip abroad. Later, still in
Paris, he wrote to Atkinson again:

> One of the most thrilling sights I have witnessed in
> a long time was the French presentation of the
> Divine Passion which was given here for ten days.
> The play had Notre-Dame Cathedral as its back-
> ground, with a great raised stage in front and a
> huge platform seating about twelve thousand specta-
> tors. A comparison with the Oberammagau presen-
> tation which I saw in 1930 was inevitable. I believe
> the French version was more picturesque, but I
> liked the German version more. The French looked
> only like Frenchmen while the Germans actually
> looked like Israelites and Romans.[30]

His love for France would never interfere with his
artistic integrity. In 1938 Countée Cullen made his final trip
to Europe. Even though the continent was now on the
brink of war, Cullen could not resist giving in to the emotions France aroused: "And what a child I am at heart, to
find myself thrilled in the same delightful way as soon as
my train reaches the outskirts of Paris. Oh, to have money
and stay here forever."[31]

Some of Countée Cullen's poems have the sound of
an impetuous and romantic boy. Cullen certainly was a

romantic poet in one sense, and this attitude probably influenced his personal life as well. But the cautious and deep thinking side of his personality guided him in his choice of a second wife. When he married Ida Mae Roberson on 27 September 1940 he had known her for ten years and had courted her for over two years before their marriage. At last he had found a good, lifelong companion and an excellent wife—a woman dedicated to him in life and, after his death, devoted to the task of collecting material about Cullen and other Negro writers.

Countée Cullen's last book of poetry, *On These I Stand*, was published posthumously in 1947. The poet, however, chose the poems to be included, for this is a collection of what he considered to be his best work. The reviews of this work will be considered in the next chapter.

Throughout his lifetime Countée Cullen stressed the desire to be considered merely a poet, not a Negro poet. He once told a New York reporter: "I want to be known as a poet and not as a Negro poet.[32] This was especially true in the 1920s when, as Arna Bontemps once wrote:

> The Negroes' gifts were still departmentalized. There were poets in the United States, and there were Negro poets. There were musicians, and there were Negro musicians. There were painters, and there were Negro painters. Cullen abhorred this attitude. Almost his only public comments about the art in which he expressed himself were pleas for an evaluation of his work strictly on its merits, without racial considerations. He was to learn, however, that this was no small matter.[33]

This was a conflicting matter never resolved, for although

Cullen wished this to be the sentiment of both reader and critic, many of the themes of his poems are strictly racial. Even Cullen once said: "Most things I write I do for the sheer love of the music in them. Somehow I find my poetry of itself treating of the Negro, of his joys and his sorrows— mostly of the latter—and of the heights and depths of emotion I feel as a Negro."[34]

His insistence on being thought of as quite simply a poet was by no means a pose or an excuse to shun the problems of the Negro in America, or to dissociate himself from any artistic endeavors made by his contemporaries. Following the Harlem riot of 1935, for example, Cullen was appointed and worked hard on a committee to investigate the riot and to suggest solutions for the situation. Harlem was, after all, his community—and he loved it. His poems were published with a great deal of frequency in two of the most active Negro journals of his day—*Crisis* and *Opportunity*—and he contributed poems to the short-lived Negro literary magazine *Fire*,[35] which was conceived by Langston Hughes and other Negro writers. After returning from his study in France (1930) Cullen gave a series of lectures, three of which directly concerned the Negro. These lectures were: "The American Negro in Literature," "Days and Nights in Harlem" (discussing the "Negro Capital," its advantages and disadvantages), and "Poetry Readings" (at which he read his own poems and those of other Negro poets.) He was generous in giving his time to read poetry at the 136th Street Branch of the New York Public Library. He also read his poems at the Race Relations Institute which he attended at Fisk University in 1944. In 1943, overcoming his distaste for propagandistic poetry, Countée Cullen wrote the following letter to the editor of a New York newspaper:

Coming home the other night from the Stage Door
Canteen where democracy is being given a chance
to prove itself with Negro and white service men
[*sic*] fraternizing as brothers in arms should, I
thought what a step backward the city of Hillburn
has taken. I think of them in this way:

> God have pity
> On such a city
> Where parent teaches child to hate;
> God look down
> On such a town
> Where Prejudice the Great
> Rules evilly
> What should be Liberty's estate.[36]

Mr. Cullen, who was described as "short, inclined to
be stocky and of medium color brown,"[37] was a sensitive,
gentle man, with a love for fun, a quiet intellectual who
developed his talent in the days when the Negro intelli-
gentsia was slowly emerging to take an active part in
American life. He spent the last twelve years of his life
teaching at the Frederick Douglass Junior High School in
New York City. Although he taught French at this school,
he did extra work with the pupils in creative writing. He
found teaching difficult at times, but he never succumbed
to the doubts that occasionally plagued him. He even re-
fused the chair of Creative Literature at Fisk University
in 1944 in order to remain where he had overcome the
initial trials of poet turned teacher.

On 10 January 1946, *The New York Times* announced
the death of Countée Cullen. (His father survived him by
only five months.) Shortly after Countée Cullen's death,
the collection of Negroana at Atlanta University changed
its name officially to the Countée Cullen Memorial Col-

lection. Its founder was his devoted friend Harold Jackman, who had been a friend to many artists in all fields. This is one of the richest collections of contemporary material by and about Negroes, including books, theater bills, clippings, concert programs, pamphlets, photographs, letters, and periodicals. There are also many of Carl Van Vechten's photographs of outstanding Negroes of the theater, art, literary, civic, and political worlds. The printers' proofs of three of Cullen's books, *The Ballad of the Brown Girl*, *Color*, and *The Lost Zoo*, are also in this famous collection.[38]

Yale University had a ceremony on 7 January 1950 marking the opening of the James Weldon Johnson Memorial Collection of Negro Arts and Letters. Carl Van Vechten was the founder who had assiduously gathered much of the material for this impressive collection. There are original manuscripts of such Cullen works as *One Way to Heaven* and *The Lost Zoo*, many typescripts of his poems, letters to and from him, and his "French Notebook." The 136th Street Branch of the New York Public Library changed its name to the Countée Cullen Branch after a small ceremony on 12 September 1951. The naming of this library in memory of the poet was an extraordinary event, for libraries had previously been named exclusively for persons who had given monetary gifts to the library. But the library board was eventually convinced of the significance of an intrinsic sort of endowment left by Countée Cullen which could never be measured in terms of money; thus, the Harlem community has a daily reminder of a man whose presence honored them.[39]

The esteem of organizations such as these was matched by the praise given to Countée Cullen by his fellow poets. William Rose Benet, in writing about him, said that "he was a true poet and wrote brave and beautiful things."[40]

And Arna Bontemps, who had recently collaborated with Cullen on a play, explained his character in this manner:

> Cullen was in many ways an old-fashioned poet. He never ventured very far from the Methodist parsonage in which he grew up in New York. A foster child, drawn into this shelter at an early age, he continued to cherish it gratefully. He paid his adopted parents a devotion, one is almost inclined to say a submission, only rarely rendered by natural sons. But it was all part of his own choice. He did not stand in fear of his foster parents. He simply preferred pleasing them to having his own way. It is possible that he felt or imagined the cords of this relationship to be the kind that would not stand strain, but the decisions he made later do not seem to support such an idea.[41]

This same devotion to family was noted by another friend and collaborator, Owen Dodson, who wrote: "If you asked his family and friends about Countée, they would tell you that he was faithful, loyal, quiet, tender."[42] The gentleness and quiet dignity so often recalled by people who knew Countée Cullen was a part of his personality apparent in much of his poetry, especially in his most characteristic lyrics. Although Countée Cullen did not entirely win his battle against being known primarily as a Negro poet, his finest poetry has always evoked the image of a man devoted to the written and spoken word, a man who could make language sing for him when he wrote with all the fire of his youthful spirit:

> Yet do I marvel at this curious thing:
> To make a poet black and bid him sing!

## NOTES

1. Stanley J. Kunitz and Howard Haycraft, *Twentieth-Century Authors* (New York: H. W. Wilson Co., 1942), pp. 336–337.

2. Frederick Asbury Cullen, *From Barefoot to Jerusalem* (n.p., n.d.), no page number.

3. Milton M. Bergerman to the author, [19] May 1969.

4. *Crisis* 23 (March 1922):219.

5. *The Magpie* 20 (November 1920):25.

6. Irving Kahn to the author, 3 June 1969.

7. *New York Times*, 2 December 1923, sec. 2, p. 1.

8. Countée Cullen to Harold Jackman, 1 July 1923, Beinecke Library, Yale University.

9. Cullen to Jackman, 25 August 1923, Beinecke Library, Yale University.

10. *Boston Chronicle*, 30 May 1925, p. 1.

11. *New York Evening World*, 1 June 1925, no page number.

12. Cullen to Carl Van Vechten, 1 October 1925, Beinecke Library, Yale University.

13. *Poetry* 28 (April 1926):50.

14. Cullen to Van Vechten, 29 April 1926, Beinecke Library, Yale University.

15. *Opportunity* 5 (September 1927):270–271.

16. *The Bookman* 46 (September 1927):103.

17. *New York Times*, 19 March 1928, p. 8.

18. *New York Herald Tribune*, 10 April 1928, no page number.

19. Cullen to Jackman, 10 August 1923, Beinecke Library, Yale University.

20. Cullen to Jackman, 18 August 1923, Beinecke Library, Yale University.

21. Cullen to Jackman, 7 April 1926, Beinecke Library, Yale University.

22. Cullen to Jackman, 28 July 1926, Beinecke Library, Yale University.

23. Ivie Jackman to the author, 7 July 1969. "On Saturday June 28, 1928, Reverend Cullen, Countée and Harold sailed for France on the Île de France at midnight—source is Harold's 1928 day book." This inquiry was made to Miss Jackman to find out if Mrs. Cullen accompanied her husband and to get the correct name of the ship on which he sailed. The *New York Times* lists the ship's sailing on the 29th—probably because of the late hour of departure.

24. Countée Cullen "French Notebook," Beinecke Library, Yale University.

25. *Saturday Review of Literature* 30 (22 March 1947):13.

26. Bynner to Cullen, 22 November 1929, in possession of Mrs. Ida Mae Cullen.

27. Typed manuscript of synopsis, boxed with *One Way to Heaven*, Beinecke Library, Yale University.

28. Stephen H. Bronz, *Roots of Negro Racial Consciousness* (New York: Libra, 1964), p. 64. This information, in part, was

taken from the *Springfield Union. See also* bibliographic entry #262 in chapter 5.

29. Cullen to Edward Atkinson, 1 August 1937, Beinecke Library, Yale University.

30. Cullen to Atkinson, 15 August 1937, Beinecke Library, Yale University.

31. Cullen to Atkinson, 2 August 1938, Beinecke Library, Yale University.

32. *Light* 3 (24 September 1927):12.

33. *Saturday Review of Literature* 30 (22 March 1947):44.

34. Jay Saunders Redding, *To Make a Poet Black* (Chapel Hill: University of North Carolina Press, 1929), p. 109.

35. This magazine did not live beyond vol. 1, no. 1, and, ironically, most of the unsold copies were destroyed in a fire.

36. Hillburn, a town in Rockland County, New York. An account of the racial problem in this place is given on page 175 in Blanche Ferguson's biography of Cullen.

37. Charles S. Johnson, "Source Material for Patterns of Negro Segregation, New York City" (n.p., Carnegie-Myrdal Study n.d.), no page number (mimeographed).

38. *Negro History Bulletin* 17 (October 1953):11–13.

39. Interview with Mrs. Dorothy Homer, Branch Librarian, Countée Cullen Branch of the New York Public Library, New York City, 1959.

40. *Saturday Review of Literature* 30 (22 March 1947):44.

41. Ibid., p. 12.

42. *Phylon* 7 (First Quarter 1946):20.

# 2

## *The Poetry of*
## *Cullen:*
## *An Explanation*

IN the June 1925 issue of *Vanity Fair*, Carl Van Vechten introduced the readers to poetry by Countée Cullen with the following statement:

> He was barely twenty-one when "The Shroud of Color" . . . created a sensation analogous to that of Edna St. Vincent Millay's *Renascence* in 1912, lifting its author at once to a position in the front ranks of contemporary American poets, white or black. . . . All his poetry is characterized by a suave, unpretentious, brittle, intellectual elegance.[1]

Soon, Countée Cullen was to receive even wider attention, for his first volume of collected poetry was published in 1925 also. The young poet's future was predicted to become successful. To help the reader understand more clearly the significance of Countée Cullen's work in modern American literature, a brief exposition of themes used, his style, his poetry in contrast with other lyric poets and other Negro poets, and a summary of reviews of his poetic works is given. It will then be possible to estimate the value of his poetry in relation to the attention he received from the literary world, and to consider the poetry for which Mr. Cullen will be remembered. The survey of reviews of his work follows in chapter 3.

Countée Cullen was primarily a lyricist, influenced by romantic poets of the nineteenth and twentieth centuries. Keats was perhaps the poet he most admired; and his most characteristic lyrics show a penchant toward writing in the style of Housman, Millay, and Edwin Arlington Robinson. Jay Saunders Redding called him the Ariel of Negro poets, one who "cannot beat the tom-tom above a faint whisper nor know the primitive delights of black rain and scarlet sun," a writer of "delightful personal love lyrics."[2] Therefore, it is not surprising to note that, besides poems concerning the race problem, Cullen's other two most constant themes were love and death. Emanuel Eisenberg explicitly cited this tendency in Cullen's poetry when his second book, *Copper Sun,* appeared. Eisenberg wrote: "In his second volume . . . Countée Cullen reveals the fatal limitations which must always restrict his expression in poetry. One-third of his poems are concerned with race, another third with love, another with death."[3]

Most of these thematic preoccupations, especially with love and death, were commented upon by an English writer also, who stated that "his poetry belongs to that which takes for its themes the love of lovely things, and the poignant sorrow for their loss in death."[4] This can be seen, for instance, in his poem "To Lovers of Earth: Fair Warning":

24

She will remain the Earth, sufficient still,
Though you are gone and with you that rare loss
That vanishes with your bewildered will.
And there shall flame no red, indignant cross
For you, no quick white scar of wrath emboss
The sky, no blood drip from a wounded moon,
And not a single star chime out of tune.

Although Cullen sang of the joy of love, as in "One Day We Played a Game," his poetry more often expressed the sorrow of love's ending, the loss of love, and the sorrow of death. Poem after poem indicates this attitude of melancholy youth, and the titles follow this pattern to make the impression indelible: "And When I Think (For One Just Dead)," "Two Thoughts of Death," "Disenchantment," "Portrait of a Lover," "Song of the Rejected Lover," "Lament," and "Variations on a Theme (The Loss of Love)." And finally, consider another of his poems on this theme, "Pity the Deep in Love":

Pity the deep in love;
They move as men asleep,
Traveling a narrow way
Precipitous and steep.
Tremulous is the lover's breath
With little moans and sighs;
Heavy are the brimming lids
Upon a lover's eyes.

The poems of Countée Cullen concerning race could fill an adequate volume, for he was involved in expressing how it felt to be a Negro from the publication of his first book, *Color*, to the publication of his last (which had, among the unpublished poems, one entitled "A Negro Mother's Lullaby"). Yet he was, and probably still is, considered the least race-conscious of the Negro poets, although—as Charles Glicksberg pointed out—he will, ironically enough, be remembered for his poems which deal with race and/or the race problem.[5] It has been said many times, for instance, that "Incident" could have been written by none other than a Negro:

> Once riding in old Baltimore,
>     Heart-filled, head-filled with glee,
> I saw a Baltimorean
>     Keep looking straight at me.
>
> Now I was eight and very small,
>     And he was no whit bigger,
> And so I smiled, but he poked out
>     His tongue, and called me, "Nigger."
>
> I saw the whole of Baltimore
> From May until December;
> Of all the things that happened there
> That's all that I remember.[6]

Cullen fought against this race consciousness to no avail; and the different reviewers wrote favorable or unfavorable criticism on this strong trait apparent in his poetry. When *Color* was published, Jessie Fauset wrote a review strongly expressing the opinion that Cullen's writing about his race produced his best poetry:

> Here I am convinced is Mr. Cullen's forte; he has
> the feeling and the gift to express coloredness in a

world of whiteness. . . . I hope he will not be de-
flected from continuing to do that of which he has
made such a brave and beautiful beginning. I hope
that no one crying down "special treatment" will
turn him from his native and valuable genre.[7]

On the other hand, this was, according to another
reviewer, a weakness which led to sentimentality, and only
when Cullen transcended this limitation did he become
"sheer poet."[8] Certainly he could not escape the fact of
being a Negro, and being a sensitive man, could not eschew
the compelling wish to say what could be expressed only
by a Negro. Babette Deutsch, in commenting on the race
theme in Cullen's work, gave a balanced and objective
appraisal:

But though one may recognize that certain of Mr.
Cullen's verses owe their being to the fact that he
shares the tragedy of his people, it must be owned
that the real virtue of his work lies in his personal
response to an experience which, however condi-
tioned by his race, is not so much racial as pro-
foundly human. The color of the mind is more
important than the color of his skin.[9]

Nevertheless, it was because of the color of his skin
that Countée Cullen was more aware of the racial problem
and could not be at all times "sheer poet." This was clearly
a problem for Cullen—wanting to write lyrics on love,
death, and beauty—always so consciously aware of his race.
This can be seen, for instance, in his poem "Uncle Jim,"
where the struggle is neatly portrayed through the young
boy, thinking of Keats, and his uncle, bitter with thoughts

of the difference between being a black man or a white man in our society:

"White folks is white," says uncle Jim;
"A platitude," I sneer;
And then I tell him so is milk,
And the froth upon his beer.

His heart walled up with bitterness,
He smokes his pungent pipe,
And nods at me as if to say,
"Young fool, you'll soon be ripe!"

I have a friend who eats his heart
Away with grief of mine,
Who drinks my joy as tipplers drain
Deep goblets filled with wine.

I wonder why here at his side,
Face-in-the-grass with him,
My mind should stray the Grecian urn
To muse on uncle Jim.

For Cullen, then, the racial problem was always there, even when one was thinking of odes by Keats, and he was impelled—*in spite of everything I can do*[10]—to write about this subject. This was the cause of much weakness in his writing, as well as some strength; for there are poems about race which have an emotional intensity that most of his white peers could not have matched.

In reading the poetry of Countée Cullen, one is often thrust back into the mid-nineteenth-century atmosphere with its romantic outbursts about love and death and nature; and his poetic vocabulary is often reminiscent of Keats and Tennyson. Countée Cullen, as a lyric poet, as a writer of sonnets, epitaphs, narratives, and short verses, was often compared to Keats. One critic, in fact, labeled him the "Keats in Labrador."[11] And Mr. Walter White, in praising him in contrast to the accomplishments by other lyric poets, wrote:

> Countée Cullen belongs to that company of lyricists of which A. E. Housman and Edna St. Vincent Millay are the bright stars. He is no mere versifier, no simple matcher of words that rhyme without meaning or feeling, no trite measurer of lines. His verse has emotional depth which is extraordinary of one of Mr. Cullen's years; he makes words hum and sing with none of the triteness and verbosity usual in a beginner. He etches his emotions and pictures with acid clearness, while underneath lies a genuine and sympathetic understanding of the joys and sorrows of life itself. All this he does with a magnificent imagery that seldom permits anything he writes to savor of the commonplace. Countée Cullen is a real poet.[12]

When asked his definition of good poetry, Cullen said that: "good poetry is a lofty thought beautifully expressed . . . poetry should not be too intellectual; it should deal more . . . with the emotion. The highest type of poem is that which warmly stirs the emotions, which awakens a responsive chord in the human heart. Poetry, like music, depends upon feeling rather than intellect, although there should of course, be enough to satisfy the mind, too."[13]

The lyrical style of Cullen most often reveals a speaker who has a touch of melancholy. Cullen, like Keats, was

impressed with the beauty, love, and joy in life; and—at the
same time—was aware of their transient quality. Both poets
continually mourned their fleetingness. Keats, in his "Ode
on Melancholy," wrote:

> She dwells with Beauty—Beauty that must die;
> And Joy, whose hand is ever at his lips
> Bidding adieu; and aching Pleasure nigh,
> Turning to poison while the bee-mouth sips:

And Cullen, expressing the passing quality of beauty, wrote:

> These are no wind-blown rumors, soft say-sos,
> No garden-whispered hearsays, lightly heard:
> I know that summer never spares the rose,
> That spring is faithless to the brightest bird.
>
> I know that nothing lovely shall prevail
> To win from Time and Death a moment's grace.
> At Beauty's birth the scythe was honed, the nai'
> Dipped for her hands, the cowl clipped from her
> face.

The evocation of a tone, achieved through revealing the
speaker's character by his emotional attitude in a given
situation, is typical of Cullen's poetry. This can be seen in
"Heritage":

> What is Africa to me:
> Copper sun or scarlet sea,
> Jungle star or jungle track,
> Strong bronzed men, or regal black
> Women from whose loins I sprang
> When the birds of Eden sang?
> *One three centuries removed*

*From the scenes his fathers loved,*
*Spicy grove, cinnamon tree.*
*What is Africa to me?*

Or, in "Wisdom Cometh with the Years":

Let me be lavish with my tears,
And dream that false is true;
Though wisdom cometh with the years,
The barren days come, too.

The expression of interrelated moods and thoughts, however, is only one way the lyricist emphasizes his compelling sentiments. Rhythm and harmony of sounds which suggest music are also important; this is especially evident in Countée Cullen's poetry. It has been noted that Cullen said he wrote poems "for the sheer love of music in them,"[14] and this musical element is an integral part of much of his poetry. When his first book was published, the reviewer in *Poetry* called it a volume of musical verse. Babette Deutsch remarked: "And even in what might be called his African poems it is Mr. Cullen's endowment of music and imagery and emotional awareness that matters, over and above the presence of jungle shapes and shadows."[15]

Consider, for instance, two stanzas from "A Song of Praise":

You have not heard my love's dark throat,
Slow-fluting like a reed,
Release the perfect golden note
She caged there for my need.

Her walk is like the replica
Of some barbaric dance

Wherein the soul of Africa
Is winged with arrogance.

Some of Cullen's poems were, indeed, set to music in
1927 by Emerson Whithorne—poems from *Color,* arranged
for voices and piano and/or chamber orchestra. One of the
poems was "Saturday's Child":

Some are teethed on a silver spoon,
With the stars strung for a rattle;
I cut my teeth as the black raccoon—
For implements of battle.

Some are swaddled in silk and down,
And heralded by a star;
They swathed my limbs in a sackcloth gown
On a night that was black as tar.

For some, godfather and goddame
The opulent fairies be;
Dame Poverty gave me my name,
And Pain godfathered me.

For I was born on Saturday—
"Bad time for planting a seed,"
Was all my father had to say,
And, "One mouth more to feed."

Death cut the strings that gave me life,
And handed me to Sorrow,
The only kind of middle wife
My folks could beg or borrow.

Abandoning the lyric style, Mr. Cullen wrote many

epitaphs for which he was considered a near master. Babette Deutsch remarked that "the twenty-eight rhymed Epitaphs [in *Color*] have, almost without exception, a pure gallic salt."[16] In these epitaphs, Cullen adopts a pose of insouciance at times, displaying most often a sharp and thrusting wit, poking fun at man's weaknesses. But sometimes there is the search for the inner man, as in "For Paul Lawrence Dunbar":

> Born of the sorrowful of heart,
> Mirth was a crown upon his head;
> Pride kept his twisted lips apart
> In jest, to hide a heart that bled.

The following epitaphs, however, are more typical.

### FOR A LADY I KNOW

> She even thinks that up in heaven
> Her class lies late and snores,
> While poor black cherubs rise at seven
> To do celestial chores.

### FOR A MOUTHY WOMAN

> God and the devil still are wrangling
> Which should have her, which repel;
> God wants no discord in his heaven;
> Satan has enough in hell.

Of his two longest narrative poems, *The Ballad of the Brown Girl* is considered to be more poetically balanced than *The Black Christ*. One critic thought *The Ballad of the Brown Girl* "placed Mr. Cullen by the side of the best modern masters of the ballad—Morris, Rossetti, and others that may be named."[17] And another critic felt that it was "an expert retelling of one of the oldest ballads of race prejudice."[18] *The Black Christ* is, first of all, a longer poem; it is more complex in subject and style, so that expressional and structural weaknesses are more easily detected. One reviewer wrote:

> There are several ways of writing down such an event as the lynching of a brother for forgetting himself so far as to share love in springtime with a white girl. It could be done with violence and bitterness, or with simple realism. Countée Cullen has visualized this episode as the mirror of the death of Christ, and of the eternal Fair Young God; he makes a religious experience of it, told to further brotherhood and faith. Yet he writes it in very "poetic" language. One has no right, perhaps, to criticize an artist's style; that is his own affair. But if it blurs the force of the experience, one is inevitably disappointed.[19]

The opening verse of *The Black Christ*, which is part of a six-verse prologue to the story, gives the reader a good foretaste of the poetic form used in the whole of this modern story of a black man's lynching:

> God's glory and my country's shame,
> And how one man who cursed Christ's name
> May never fully expiate
> That crime till at the Blessed Gate
> Of Heaven He meet and pardon me
> Out of His love and charity;
> How God, who needs no man's applause,

For love of my stark soul, of flaws
Composed, seeing it slip, did stoop
Down to the mire and pick me up,
And in the hollow of His hand
Enact again at my command
The world's supremest tragedy,
Until I die my burthen be;
How Calvary in Palestine,
Extending down to me and mine,
Was but the first leaf in a line
Of trees on which a Man should swing
World without end, in suffering
For all men's healing, let me sing.

The alert reader is immediately aware of the poet's weakness for relying on expressions which are not so much a part of his creation as they are a part of literature already written, and then using them to no great effectiveness. Notice the opening line, "God's glory and my country's shame" and, then, the last two lines of this passage, "World without end, in suffering/For all men's healing, let me sing."

The greatest faults in expression, however, are evident in the speeches Cullen gives the hero, Jim. At one point he says: "We never seem to reach nowhere"; then, "Likely there ain't no God at all." We believe in this Jim. Yet, one verse further, he expresses himself in this manner:

"I have a fear," he used to say,
"This thing [lynching] may come to me some day.
Some man contemptuous of my race
And its lost rights in this hard place,
Will strike me down for being black . . ."

Here the poet has confused the reader with a double image

of the hero: first, Jim the simple, semiliterate boy; then, Jim, the highly literate seer. Clearly, Cullen is imposing his own poetic talent on a boy meant to have less agility with the English language than the poet writing the narrative. The reviewer in *Opportunity* pointed out this same weakness, contrasting the phrase "We never seem to reach nowhere," with the "sickly poetic speech"—"Twere best, I think, we moved away." The reviewer went on to say: "No person ever spoke like this today; and when the same character is pursued by lynchers, face bloodied, delivers a speech to his family, almost seven pages long, in this same false diction, instead of escaping from the lynchers, the end becomes grotesquely unnatural."[20]

Cullen's other long narrative, *The Ballad of the Brown Girl*, was a retelling of an old story, written, with the exception of two verses, in quatrains. This poem was generally well received by the critics. Although this, too, was a poem about racial prejudice, Cullen treated the tale with objectivity and avoided obscuring the poem's meaning with his own feelings. Some of Cullen's shorter verses adopt a narrative form, such as "Incident," "Simon the Cyrenian Speaks," "Two Who Crossed a Line," and "Red":

### RED

She went to buy a brand new hat,
And she was ugly, black and fat:
"This red becomes you well," they said,
And placed it high upon her head.
And then they laughed behind her back
To see it glow against the black.
She paid for it with regal mien,
And walked out proud as any queen.

36

The line between the narrative and the lyric in many of Countée Cullen's shorter verses is, however, difficult to find. Essentially, Cullen was a lyricist who often introduced the narrative element in his poetry in order to strengthen the emotional impact of the whole poem. It was this lyric-cum-narrative quality in Cullen's poetry that made critics continually compare him to such poets as A. E. Housman and Edwin Arlington Robinson.

Cullen's penchant towards lyricism, coupled with his personal admiration for the poet made it inevitable that Cullen and Keats would be compared. In his review of *Copper Sun,* E. Merrill Root commented: "Countée Cullen loves Keats; therefore he will know what I mean—and how much I mean —when I say that in his sensuous richness of phrase, in his death-shadowed joy, he reminds me of Keats."[21]

Both Keats and Cullen wrote numerous poems about love, death, a love of beauty in nature, and "death-shadowed joy"; and it is perhaps in this type of poetry that the influence of Keats on Cullen can be seen most clearly. At the parting of lovers, Keats wrote:

> Think not of it, sweet one, so;—
> Give it not a tear;
> Sigh thou mayest, and bid it go
> Any—any where.
>
> Do not look so sad, sweet one,—
> Sad and fadingly;
> Shed one drop, then it is gone,
> Oh 'twas born to die.

Cullen, in his poem "At Parting," evokes the same sort of attitude in his narrator—asking his loved one to remember that "All stories may not boast a happy end./Love was a flower, sweet, and flowers fade;/Love was a fairy tale; these have their close . . ."

The word death appears frequently in the work of these two poets, more often, however, in Cullen's verses. Keats was more subtle in his expression of the presence of death, and he (in contrast to Cullen) wrote more poems about joy, without the overshadowing awareness of death. Even though death ends both joy and sorrow for the speakers in the poems of Keats and Cullen, death for both of them is an awakening not to be feared. Notice "On Death" by Keats:

> Can death be sleep, when life is but a dream,
>   And scenes of bliss pass as a phantom by?
> The transient pleasures as a vision seem,
>   And yet we think the greatest pain's to die
>
> . . . . . . . .
>
> How strange it is that man on earth should roam,
>   And lead a life of woe, but not forsake
> His rugged path; nor dare he view alone
>   His future doom which is but to awake.

Indeed, for Cullen, death is often a relief; or, if not that, at least better than some things that must be endured in life—such as the loss of love:

> I have no will to weep or sing,
> No least desire to pray or curse;
> The loss of love is a terrible thing;
> They lie who say that death is worse.

And the fear men have of death:

Dead men are wisest, for they know
How far the roots of flowers go,
How long a seed must rot to grow.

. . . . . . . .

Strange, men should flee their company,
Or think me strange who long to be
Wrapped in their cool immunity.

This protective aspect of death (a Protestant death, without
the worry of Purgatory), found in many poems by Cullen,
was a belief of Keats and is revealed through some of his
longer poems. (In "The Fall of Hyperion," there are the
lines: "Oftentimes I pray'd/Intense, that Death would take
me from the vale/And all its burthens.") Cullen's expression
of the relief brought by death is beautifully portrayed in
his "Death to the Poor":

In death alone is what consoles; and life
And all its end is death; and that fond hope
Whose music like a mad fantastic fife
Compels us up this ridged and rocky slope.
Through lightning, hail, and hurt of human look,
Death is the vibrant light we travel toward,
The mystic Inn forepromised in the Book
Where all are welcomed in to bed and board.

An angel whose star-banded fingers hold
The gift of dreams and calm, ecstatic sleep
In easier beds than those we had before,
Death is the face of God, the only fold
That pens content and ever-happy sheep,
To paradise the only open door.

It was not only in theme that these two poets resembled each other: Cullen, like Keats, loved colorful words. "Color with Keats is likely to be indicated by terms that imply richness and massiveness of substance—gold and silver, marble and bronze—or rich luxuriousness of fabric."[22] Cullen's use of colorful words was most often in the traditional mode ("nut-brown maiden," "milk-white maiden," "golden splendor of the day"), but they were descriptively rich—with an emotional intensity to match the specific words of color. Note, for instance, two passages from *The Ballad of the Brown Girl*:

> The Brown Girl came to him as might
> A queen to take her crown;
> With gems her fingers flamed and flared;
> Her robe was weighted down.
>
> Her hair was black as sin is black
> And ringed about with fire;
> Her eyes were black as night is black
> When moon and stars conspire;
> Her mouth was one red cherry clipt
> In twain, her voice a lyre.
>
> . . . . . . . .
>
> Her skin was white as almond milk
> Slow trickling from the flower;
> Her frost-blue eyes were darkening
> Like clouds before a shower;
>
> Her thin pink lips were twin rosebuds
> That had not come to flower,
> And crowning all, her golden hair
> Was loosened out in shower.

The luxuriant verses of Keats are richer and fuller:

> She was a gordian shape of dazzling hue,
> Vermillion—spotted, golden, green, and blue;
> Striped like a zebra, freckled like a pard,
> Eyed like a peacock, and all crimson barr'd;
> And full of silver moons, that, as she breathed,
> Dissolv'd, or brighter shone, or interwreathed
> Their lustres with the gloomier tapestries—

This show of color in the poetry of Keats greatly attracted Cullen, although he did not use colors with the same force or variety as did his admired poet. Cullen, with great frequency, employed the colors red, scarlet, or gold. In contrast, and of necessity in his race poems, he achieved some facility enriching his poetry with black and white and some synonyms (e.g., ebony) for these two words. That John Keats, however, was a constant source of inspiration to Cullen can be seen in the concluding lines of his poem, "To John Keats, Poet. At Springtime":

> "John Keats is dead," they say, but I
> Who hear your full insistent cry
> In bud and blossom, leaf and tree,
> Know John Keats still writes poetry.
> And while my head is earthward bowed
> To read new life spring from your shroud,
> Folks seeing me must think it strange
> That merely sprung should so derange
> My mind. They do not know that you,
> John Keats, keep revel with me, too.

Countée Cullen's poetry also bears a close resemblance to both the poetry of Edward Arlington Robinson (whom

Cullen considered to be America's finest poet),[23] and of Edna St. Vincent Millay. Robinson's influence is obvious in some of Cullen's lyrical narratives such as "The Street Called Crooked," "One Day I Told My Love," "Simon the Cyrenian Speaks," and "Judas Iscariot." Also, comparison of Cullen's "Two Who Crossed a Line (She Crosses)" with Robinson's "Miniver Cheevy" reveals a marked similarity in theme and treatment. Although Cullen's approach is more serious, lacking the underlying ironic humor present in the Robinson verse, the poems are worth noting together. Cullen undoubtedly sensed in Robinson the sort of Puritanism both poets never abandoned in their writings. A religious faith, tempered by skepticism, is implicit in the poetry of Robinson and Cullen (who probably could not escape this stance because of his religious upbringing). And they shared the optimistic opinion that, beneath man's troubles (the ones inflicted on him, the ones he inflicts on himself), man could find something in which to hope. As F. J. Mather said of Robinson, there was "along with this tragic sense of life a wistful and expectant hopefulness."[24] One might substitute melancholy for tragic in the case of Cullen, and the quote would be strikingly applicable.

The most noticeable example of the impression made upon Cullen by Miss Millay is his "The Shroud of Color." Here, the poet expresses the burden and the sometimes unbearable strain of being a black man in this world, of the wish for death to end his troubles, but of his ultimate recovery of courage to find and to pursue his place in the world. Cullen, with one exception ("To the Swimmer"), did not write free verse or use experimental forms; Miss Millay, also, seldom ventured from traditional poetical forms. But the resemblances between the poetry of these two lyricists goes further. There is, in the poetry of both

Miss Millay and Cullen, a singing about the passing moment, the bittersweet of love and of its transiency, an almost childlike grief in the knowledge of death, and an overall tone of naïveté. This is true of many of Miss Millay's earlier poems, for her development as a poet can be divided into periods; and the similarity between these two poets lessens with Miss Millay's maturation. It is, therefore, best to look for the parallelism between the two poets in the early poetry of Miss Millay.

In contrast to Miss Millay's "Renascence," Cullen's "The Shroud of Color" begins:

> "Lord, being dark," I said, "I cannot bear
> The further touch of earth, the scented air;
> Lord, being dark, forewilled to that despair
> My color shrouds me in, I am as dirt
> Beneath my brother's heel; there is a hurt
> In all the simple joys which to a child
> Are sweet; they are contaminate, defiled
> By truths of wrongs the childish vision fails
> To see; too great a cost this birth entails.
> I strangle in this yoke drawn tighter than
> The worth of bearing it, just to be a man.
> I am not brave enough to pay the price
> In full; I lack the strength to sacrifice . . .

For Cullen, the oppressiveness is caused by the burden of color—"My color shrouds me in"—whereas the onus for the speaker in "Renascence" is caused by a discovery of the world's grief and an awareness of an innate complexity in the universe:

> Over these things I could not see:
> These were the things that bounded me.

And I could touch them with my hand,
Almost, I thought, from where I stand!
And all at once things seemed so small
The breath came short, and scarce at all.

. . . . . . .

I saw and heard, and knew at last
The How and Why of all things past,
And present, and forevermore.
The Universe, cleft to the core,
Lay open to my probing sense,
That, sickening, I would fain pluck thence
But could not,—nay! but needs must suck
At the great wound, and could not pluck
My lips away till I had drawn
All venom out.—Ah, fearful pawn:
For my omniscience paid I toll
In infinite remorse of soul.

In the poem by Cullen, after the speaker declares an inability
to stand the pressure of living in the world as a black man,
the narrator asks:

. . . Lord, let me die.

Across the earth's warm, palpitating crust
I flung my body in embrace; I thrust
My mouth into the grass and sucked the dew,
Then gave it back in tears my anguish drew;
So hard I pressed against the ground, I felt
The smallest sandgrain like a knife, and smelt
The next year's flowering; all this to speed
My body's dissolution, fain to feed
The worms. And so I groaned, and spent my strength

> Until, all passion spent, I lay full length
> And quivered like a flayed and bleeding thing.

Notice, besides the preparation for death, the heavy sexual overtones of the narrator. The language is suggestive of a comparison between the love act/death versus oppression/ death, intermingled with the underlying question of what God expects man to do in such a world. Although Cullen and Miss Millay had their respective poems published when they had reached the same age (she had been nineteen, he, twenty), there is none of this sensuality in the Millay poem. In "Renascence" there is also the death wish:

> And so beneath the weight lay I
> And suffered death, but could not die.

But then the wish is fulfilled:

> Long had I lain thus, craving death,
> When quietly the earth beneath
> Gave way, and inch by inch, so great
> At last had grown the crushing weight,
> Into the earth I sank till I
> Full six feet under ground did lie,
> And sank no more,—there is no weight
> Can follow here, however great.
> From off my breast I felt it roll,
> And as it went my tortured soul
> Burst forth and fled in such a gust
> That all about me swirled the dust.

The sinking into the earth by the narrator of "Renascence" has its parallel in "The Shroud of Color" where the black man is lifted toward the heavens:

So lay till lifted on a great black wing
That had no mate nor flesh-apparent trunk
To hamper it; with me all time had sunk
Into oblivion; when I awoke
The wing hung poised above two cliffs that broke
The bowels of the earth in twain, and cleft
The seas apart. Below, above, to left,
To right, I saw what no man saw before:
Earth, hell, and heaven; sinew, vein, and core.

The escape from earth is longer and more tortured for
the speaker in Cullen's poem. In "Renascence" there is a
poignant recapturing of what was formerly good to experience: the patter of the rain, the "freshened, fragrant breeze/
From drenched and dripping apple-trees"; and the wish for
a return to life is nearly immediate. But the narrator in "The
Shroud of Color" must view heaven and earth, see Lucifer's
fall, must be given a lesson in man's weakness:

> . . . but still the clod
> In me was sycophant unto the rod,
> And cried, "Why mock me thus? Am I a god?

Still, the narrator is given a chance to relinquish his cow-
ardly death-wish: he is shown the courage of other black
men who, despite the trials of living, have courage to
struggle on. The narrator, then ashamed of his cowardice
and weakness, states:

> The cries of all dark people near or far
> Were billowed over me, a mighty surge
> Of suffering in which my puny grief must merge
> And lose itself; I had no further claim to urge
> For death . . .

For both narrators, the return to life is a renewal of faith in God and an acceptance to be a part, once more, of the natural world. This mood is strong in "Renascence" where the narrator says:

> I know the path that tells Thy way
> Through the cool eve every day;
> God, I can push the grass apart
> And lay my fingers on Thy heart!
>
> .  .  .  .  .  .  .
>
> The soul can split the sky in two,
> And let the face of God shine through.
> But East and West will pinch the heart
> That can not keep them pushed apart;
> And he whose soul is flat—the sky
> Will cave in on him by and by.

The ending in both poems show a reconciliation with the grief that is in the world and a willingness to make an effort to see the joy as well as the sorrow in it. In "The Shroud of Color" the narrator's return to the living world is joyful and his vision is now clear:

> Right glad I was to stoop to what I once
>     had spurned,
> Glad even unto tears; I laughed aloud;
>     I turned
> Upon my back, and through the tears for joy
>     would run,
> My sight was clear; I looked and saw the rising
>     sun.

The similarity of experience in these two poems is heightened by the poetic outbursts that express the spirit of

the young, serious persons they were when they wrote
these poems. Cullen, like Edna St. Vincent Millay, often
expressed an experience, say a thought of death, with a
childlike poignancy; and his love of beauty in the world
was often an overpowering emotion, as it was for Miss
Millay in "God's World":

> O World, I cannot hold thee close enough!
>
> . . . . . . . .
>
> Long have I known a glory in it all,
>   But never knew I this:
>   Here such a passion is
> As stretcheth me apart,—Lord, I do fear
> Thou'st made the world too beautiful this year;
> My soul is all but out of me,—let fall
> No burning leaf; prithee, let no bird call.

And Cullen, in "To John Keats, Poet. At Springtime":

> I cannot hold my peace, John Keats,
> I am as helpless in the toil
> Of Spring as any lamb that bleats
> To feel the solid earth recoil
> Beneath his puny legs. Spring beats
> Her tocsin call to those who love her,
> And lo! the dogwood petals cover
> Her breast with drifts of snow, and sleek
> White gulls fly screaming to her, and hover
> About her shoulders, and kiss her cheek,
> While white and purple lilacs muster
> A strength that bears them to a cluster
> Of color and odor; for her sake
> All things that slept are now awake.

The resemblances in the poetry of Cullen and Millay are greatest in the earliest poems of both these poets. As Miss Millay developed poetically, she was able to adopt a less serious attitude toward love and other problems in life than was Cullen; and, despite the weaknesses in her propagandistic poetry (such the "The Murder of Lidice"), Miss Millay was able to give a freshness to emotional experiences in a manner never achieved by Cullen in his later poetry.

The difficulty of comparing Cullen with other Negro poets stems from the fact of his being a lyricist who followed the traditional pattern of the old and new romantic poets. Had Cullen been enrolled in an all-Negro high school, his poetry might have been more Negro in tone. Still, this is speculative; given his same nature, he may have written just as he did. In any case, among the Negro poets, Cullen has been compared with Joseph Cotter, Jr.,[25] and William Stanley Braithwaite.[26] Inasmuch as Cullen and Langston Hughes were probably the two most outstanding Negro poets in the United States during the 1920s and the 1930s, it is inevitable that comparisons have been made. (Hughes was born in 1902.) One writer summed up their differences by saying:

> Cullen . . . is not that man of common clay identified with those far down as is his contemporary. . . . Langston Hughes is concerned with the Negro who is holding up the lamp post, scrubbing door knobs, cleaning floors, or banging on the ebony keys of a piano in the back of a cabaret. Countée Cullen is mainly concerned with the charms and the beauties appreciated by the higher social strata.[27]

The words "higher social strata" are not quite accurate. The writer would have been more just, and correct, in saying the higher intellectual strata; for it has been noted that Cullen's poems are more intellectual and less spontaneous than those of Hughes.[28] And on the surface, Mr. Cullen is bound less by the color of his skin than Mr. Hughes, although this is true in fewer cases than is generally conceded. One of the best discussions of Hughes and Cullen was written by Arna Bontemps, who described the two poets in this fashion:

> Except for their ages (there was a difference of about one year) and the fact that each was a Negro American, they were not much alike. An observer got the impression that while they were drawn together by the common experience of writing poetry, they actually had remarkably little in common. Their attitudes, their tastes and preferences—everything one saw in their personalities was different. Cullen's verses skip; those by Hughes glide. But in life Hughes is the merry one. Cullen was a worrier. . . . Equally evident, then as later, was Cullen's tendency to get his inspiration, his rhythms and patterns as well as much of his substance from books and the world lore of scholarship; while Hughes made a ceremony of standing in the deck of a tramp steamer and tossing into the sea, one by one, all the books he had accumulated before his twenty-first birthday.[29]

There was a conflict between their aims, their philosophies of poetry. In Cullen's review of "The Weary Blues," he is frank in his criticism, and this serves to illustrate a basic difference between the two poets: "I regard the jazz poems as interlopers in the company of the truly beautiful poems in other sections of the book. . . . I wonder if jazz poems really belong to that dignified company, that select and austere circle of high literary expression which we call poetry."[30]

Countée Cullen was a unique Negro poet, partly because of his upbringing and schooling, partly because of his preoccupation with verse in a formalistic sense. One influenced the other, naturally; but this uniqueness separated him from his black brothers. In any case, comparing poets on the basis of skin color can be misleading and unfruitful. If Cullen closely resembles another poet of his race, one might—almost without question—find the poet in the anthology of poems edited by Cullen himself, *Caroling Dusk*.


## NOTES

1. *Vanity Fair* 24 (June 1925):62.

2. Jay Saunders Redding, *To Make a Poet Black* (Chapel Hill: University of North Carolina Press, 1939), p. 111.

3. *The Bookman* 46 (September 1927):103.

4. Winifred Knox, "American Negro Poetry," *The Bookman* 81 (London, October 1931):16.

5. Charles I. Glicksberg, "Negro Poets and the American Tradition," *Antioch Review* 6 (Summer 1946):246.

6. As for this poem, it is not based on any definite occurrence in Countée Cullen's life, as many would like to be-

lieve. It is merely a poem which illustrates a believable situation in a likely city. Cullen's widow has confirmed this statement.

7. *Crisis* 31 (March 1926):238.

8. *New York Times Book Review*, 21 August 1927, p. 5.

9. *Nation* 121 (30 December 1925):764.

10. *New York Times*, 2 December 1923, sec. 2, p. 1.

11. *Opportunity* 5 (September 1927):270.

12. Undated clipping, source unknown: Countée Cullen vertical file, Moorland Room, Howard University, Washington, D.C.

13. Winifred Rothermel, "Countée Cullen Sees Future for the Race," *St. Louis Argus*, 3 February 1928.

14. Redding, *To Make a Poet Black*, p. 109.

15. *Nation* 121 (30 December 1925):764.

16. Ibid.

17. *Opportunity* 4 (May 1926):163.

18. *Poetry* 70 (July 1947):223.

19. Ibid. 35 (February 1930):288.

20. *Opportunity* 7 (March 1930):93.

21. Ibid. 5 (September 1927):270.

22. Joseph Warren Beach, *A Romantic View of Poetry* (Minneapolis: University of Minnesota Press, 1944), p. 13.

23. "Countée Cullen Poet By Accident," *Baltimore Afro-American*, 29 March 1930.

24. *Saturday Review of Literature* 6 (11 January 1930): 629.

25. Lloyd G. Oxley, "The Black Man in World Literature," *Philadelphia Tribune*, 27 May 1937.

26. Redding, *To Make a Poet Black*, p. 108.

27. "Negro Poets, Singers in the Dawn," *Negro History Bulletin* 2 (November 1938):15.

28. Oxley, "The Black Man in World Literature."

29. Arna Bontemps, "The Harlem Renaissance," *Saturday Review of Literature* 30 (22 March 1947):12.

30. *Opportunity* 4 (February 1926):73.

# 3

# Contemporary Reviews
of Cullen's Work

THE major collections of poetry by
Countée Cullen were *Color* (1925), *Copper Sun* (1927),
*The Black Christ* (1929), *The Medea, and Some Poems*
(1935), and *On These I Stand* (1947). It is not my inten-
tion to examine at considerable length the reviews of these
books; but excerpts from some will aid in considering
Cullen's reputation and will also shed some light on his
development as a poet.

*Color* was received with a great deal of praise and
admiration. Whatever awkwardness present in some poems
("it has the faults of youth," said Babette Deutsch)[1] was
considered insignificant when compared with his fine ear
for lyric passages. One reviewer ventured this statement:
"If there is a more promising poet in America, I do not
know his name. These people who feel that genius dips
back into the centuries will have a hard time explaining
this twenty-two year old boy. Countée Cullen is a supreme
master of Beauty."[2]

Many reviewers touched on the significance of race in this first book but, in general, decided that its great importance to Cullen did not overshadow his pure lyrics. The reviewer in *Poetry* wrote:

> Perhaps the distinctive quality of this poet's work is of some racial significance, but such a speculation is hardly relevant here. Much can be said about the unique interest of Mr. Cullen's book as a personal document; but this is a general rather than a special interest, and has already been widely emphasized.[3]

This same opinion was shared by the reviewer in *World Tomorrow* who wrote: "In a considerable proportion of his verse his themes justify his title; but nevertheless his outlook is universal."[4]

A dissenting viewpoint was voiced by the reviewer in *Crisis* who, however, found Cullen's racial poetry the most significant in the book:

> "Color" is the name of Mr. Cullen's book and color is, rightly, in every sense its prevailing characteristic. For not only does every bright glancing abound in color but it is also in another sense the yard-stick by which all the work in this volume is to be measured. Thus his poems fall into three categories: Those, and there are very few, in which no mention is made of color; those in which the adjectives "black" or "brown" or "ebony" are deliberately introduced to show that the type which the author had in mind was not white; and thirdly the poems which arise out of the consciousness of being a "Negro in a day like this" in America.[5]

*Copper Sun* was generally less favorably received. Harry Alan Potamkin wrote: "Between 'Color' and 'Copper Sun,' Countée Cullen has grown two years older. He has not, however, come any nearer to a realization of the constituents of his talent nor their proper combinations. His poetry begins and ends in an epithet skill."[6] And the same reviewer, in writing of Cullen's race consciousness, commented:

> Mr. Cullen has capitalized the fact of race without paying for such capitalization by the exploitation of the material and essence of race. Once race becomes to him more than capital and its poetic form more than the statement of its fact, he will create, upon what are undoubtedly unusual gifts, poems of import.[7]

On the other hand, *The New York Times* book reviewer wrote: "It is encouraging to observe that it reveals a profounder depth than 'Color.' "[8] And Cullen received a letter from Edwin Arlington Robinson in which the other poet wrote:

> I have your new book . . . which came to me through your publishers, and I am glad to tell you that it has given me a great deal of pleasure and satisfaction. There is something in your work that makes it entirely your own. You may remember that your first book made a similar impression on me.[9]

After Countée Cullen returned from his sojourn of study and writing in France, his fourth book of poetry—

*The Black Christ*—appeared (*The Ballad of the Brown Girl* preceded this). The critical opinion was divided on this emotional narrative tale. It was warmly received by *The New York Times* reviewer who wrote: "Cullen does not make his black martyr a second Christ. But in the simplicity of his verse there is enmeshed more of significance and beauty than will be found in many a day."[10]

But the reviewer in *Opportunity* did not see that Cullen had advanced significantly, and the weakness of this volume cited by the *Nation* reviewer was that the title poem lacked "clarity of conception."[11] The *Times* (London) reviewer, however, was favorably impressed. The longest review of *The Black Christ* appeared in the magazine *Poetry*. There, the reviewer summed up her criticism by stating: "The same practice of poetic law and manner that makes the briefer poems in this volume pleasant and musical and slight prevents this long poem from seeming to have a style as simple, devout and important as its theme."[12]

In 1935 Cullen's *The Medea, and Some Poems*, was published and received the most favorable reviews of any book of poetry by Cullen since the publication of *Color*. Philip Blair Rice, in his enthusiasm, wrote: "Where Oxford dons have so often failed, an American Negro has succeeded. . . . The result is a very forceful and poignant recreation of the story."[13]

But Mr. Rice did not discuss the poems which another critic felt to be too closely related to the genteel tradition, although "the verse has some poise and charm and occasional flashes of emotional sincerity."[14] The reviewer in *Opportunity* discussed the poetry more fully and made note of the fine sonnets included in this collection. In general, the reviewers felt that Cullen was at last beginning to fulfill the promise of his early talent.

The next important book of poetry by Cullen, however, appeared after his death. It was impossible to tell
whether or not this feeling of the reviewers had been correct, because *On These I Stand* contained selections from
Cullen's previously published books. Therefore, most reviewers used this final volume of poetry to estimate the
progress that Cullen had made between 1925 and 1945. The
general opinion was one of disappointment, a feeling one
reviewer believed Cullen himself to have felt when he
compiled the volume.[15] This reviewer traced Cullen's literary career from the publication of *Color* to that of *On
These I Stand,* and singled out *Color, The Ballad of the
Brown Girl,* and *The Medea* as the best books of his collected poetry. In trying to reach a conclusion concerning
why Cullen's promise "faded into mediocre fulfillment,"
this reviewer wrote: "Cullen neither accepted nor developed a comprehensive world-view. As a consequence, his
poems seem to result from occasional impulses rather than
from direction by an integrated individual. . . . He was, in
other words, an able and perplexed intelligence and a sensitive and confused heart."[16]

John Ciardi wrote that Cullen's weakness came from a
"taint of 'artiness' "; but he also pointed out the poet's
strength in writing sonnets, sensitive lyrics, and "his varia-
tion of the 'made ballad' (as opposed to the 'artless ballad')."[17] Cullen's muse had, as far as the reviewers were
concerned, deserted him too soon and for too long a time.
As Arna Bontemps expressed it: "Cullen did not live to see
another springtime resurgence of his own creative powers
comparable with the impulse that produced the first three
books of poetry, the books which give his selected poems
most of their lilt and brightness."[18]

Although Countée Cullen never fulfilled the promise

of his brilliant beginning, he was a poet—whatever his weak-nesses—who never completely lost his lyric touch. To be termed a "minor poet" is still to be a poet.

It is evident, even from these selected reviews, that Countée Cullen received a great deal of attention from critics. He was not an insignificant figure in American literature. His first book of poetry secured a niche in the vast body of poetic literature which has been published in modern America. It does not seem plausible that critics would have so seriously concerned themselves with a poet—Negro or white—unless there was something of value in his poetry. The adverse reviews, then, and the general opinion of critics that Cullen did not exhibit a marked advance in his poetry does not at all cancel out the value of his better poems. There are among his verses—as has been pointed out—those which could only have been written by a Negro of Cullen's sensitiveness and creative abilities. It is, there-fore, for poems such as "Incident," "Heritage," "Threnody for a Brown Girl," "The Shroud of Color," and *The Ballad of the Brown Girl*; for his skillful epitaphs, and for some of his sonnets, that Countée Cullen will certainly be remembered.

## NOTES

1. *Nation* 121 (30 December 1925):764.

2. *International Book Review* 4 (March 1926):252.

3. *Poetry* 28 (April 1926):53.

4. *World Tomorrow* 8 (November 1925):353.

5. *Crisis* 31 (March 1926):238.

6. *New Republic* 52 (12 October 1927):218.

7. Ibid.

8. *New York Times Book Review*, 21 August 1927, p. 5.

9. Robinson to Cullen, 4 September 1927. (In Cullen's personal scrapbook, in the possession of his widow.)

10. *New York Times Book Review*, 1 December 1929, p. 7.

11. *Nation* 130 (12 March 1930):303.

12. *Poetry* 35 (February 1930):289.

13. *Nation* 141 (18 September 1935):336.

14. *New Republic* 85 (25 December 1935):208.

15. *Poetry* 70 (July 1947):223.

16. Ibid.

17. *Atlantic Monthly* 179 (March 1947):145.

18. Arna Bontemps, "The Harlem Renaissance," *Saturday Review of Literature* 30 (22 March 1947):44.

# PART II

# Bibliography

# 4

# *Major Writings of Cullen*

*THIS* chapter lists the major writings of Countée Cullen under the following headings: *collected poetry* (including the anthology he edited), the entries of which are annotated, and a list of reviews follows the annotation; *articles* (including book reviews); *poems in periodicals; miscellaneous works; recorded works;* and *unpublished works.* The arrangement of these entries is alphabetical with the exception of the books of collected poems and the series of "The Dark Tower" articles which are arranged according to the date of publication.

## COLLECTED POETRY

1. *Color.* New York: Harper & Brothers, 1925.
   This is the first book of collected poems by Cullen. These poems—many by far his best—are full of a youthful and exploratory spirit. Many

of the poems, such as "Heritage," "Incident," and "The Shroud of Color," deal with racial themes, as the title suggests.

## Reviews

*Akron* (Ohio) *Beacon Journal*, 8 January 1926.

*Baltimore Evening Sun*, 19 December 1925.

*Birmingham Herald*, 29 August 1926.

*Birmingham News*, 20 December 1925.

*Booklist* 22 (February 1926):200.

*The Bookman* 62 (December 1925):503. Reviewer: John Farrar.

*Boston Evening Transcript*, 15 April 1926.

*Brooklyn Citizen*, 20 December 1925. Reviewer: Gremin Zorn.

*Brooklyn Daily Eagle*, 14 November 1925.

*Chicago Post*, 24 December 1925. Reviewer: Llewellyn Jones.

*Christian Advocate*, 31 December 1925.

*Christian Century* 42 (24 December 1925):1611. Reviewer: Paul Hutchinson.

*Cleveland Open Shelf*, January 1926, p. 5.

*Commonweal* (3 March 1926):472. Reviewer: Thomas Walsh.

*Contemporary Verse*, January 1926. Reviewer: Madeline Mason-Manheim.

*Crisis* 31 (March 1926):238–239. Reviewer: Jessie Fauset.

*Critical Review*, March 1926, p. 7. Reviewer: Martin Russak.

*Detroit News*, 17 January 1926. Reviewer: Al Weeks.

*Dial* 80 (February 1926):161.

*Harvard Crimson*, 31 October 1925. Reviewer: Cornelius DuBois.

*Independent* 115 (7 November 1925):539.

*Indianapolis News*, 20 January 1926.

*International Book Review* 4 (March 1926):252. Reviewer: Jim Tully.

*Los Angeles Record*, 4 January 1926.

*Lynchburg* (Va.) *News*, 17 January 1926.

*Lyric West* 5 (n.d.):211. Reviewer: Lois Burton Moon.

*Nashville Tennessean*, 11 April 1926.

*Nation* 121 (30 December 1925):763. Reviewer: Babette Deutsch.

*New Republic* 46 (31 March 1926):179. Reviewer: Eric Walrond.

*New York Evening Post*, 30 January 1926 Reviewer: Charles Norman.

*New York Herald Tribune,* 10 January 1926. Reviewer: Mark Van Doren.

*New York New Leader*, 24 April 1926.

*New York Sun*, 23 January 1926. Reviewer: Joseph Auslander.

*New York Times*, 8 November 1925, sec. 8, p. 15. Reviewer: Herbert S. Gorman.

*Newark Evening News*, 20 February 1926.

*Northwestern Christian Advocate*, 19 November 1925.

*Oklahoma City Oklahoman*, 11 April 1926. Reviewer: B. A. Botkin.

*Opportunity* 4 (January 1926):14. Reviewer: Alain Locke.

———— (May 1926):163–164. Reviewer: Robert T. Kerlin.

*Palms* 3 (January 1926):121–123.

*Philadelphia Record*, 26 June 1926. Reviewer: Dorothy Kahn.

*Pittsburgh Courier*, 23 January 1926, p. 16. Reviewer: Houron Temple.

*Poetry* 28 (April 1926):50–53. Reviewer: George H. Dillon.

*Pratt Institute Quarterly Booklist*, Spring 1926, p. 26.
*San Francisco Chronicle*, 13 December 1925.
*Saturday Review of Literature* 2 (13 February 1926):556.
*Times* (London), 21 January 1926.
*Toronto Saturday Night*, 27 February 1926.
*Tulsa World*, 30 June 1926. Reviewer: Inez Callaway.
*Vogue* 67 (May 1926):144. Reviewer: Berenice C. Skidelsky.
*World Tomorrow* 8 (November 1925):353.
*Xenia* (Ohio) *Evening Gazette*, 10 July 1926.
*Yale Review* 15 (July 1926):824. Reviewer: Clement Wood.

2. *Copper Sun.* New York: Harper & Brothers, 1927.

> Most of the poems in this book concern love, death, or the race problem. The concentration on these themes often limits the poet's expression; and his inclination toward the studied and bookish phrase often strains the emotional element. Even so, the poetic talent of Cullen cannot be denied when reading such poems as "To Lovers of Earth: Fair Warning" and "Threnody for a Brown Girl."

*Reviews*

*Booklist* 24 (November 1927):59.
*The Bookman* 66 (September 1927):103. Reviewer: Emanuel Eisenberg.
*Boston Guardian*, 29 October 1927.
*Boston Transcript*, 27 August 1927, p. 2.
*Buffalo Times*, 31 July 1927.
*Chicago Defender*, 31 December 1927. Reviewer: Blanche Watson.

*Chicago Journal of Commerce*, 26 November 1927.
*Cincinnati Commercial Tribune*, 31 July 1927.
*Cleveland Open Shelf,* December 1927, p. 133.
*Columbus* (Ohio) *Dispatch,* 31 July 1927.
*Critical Review*, March 1928, p. 7. Reviewer: Martin Russak.
*Hartford Courant*, 31 July 1927.
*Independent* 119 (9 September 1927):314–315.
*Nation* 125 (9 November 1927):518. Reviewer: Herbert S. Gorman.
*New Republic* 52 (12 October 1927):218. Reviewer: Harry Alan Potamkin.
*New York Amsterdam News*, 26 October 1927. Reviewer: Mary White Ovington.
*New York Herald Tribune Books*, 21 August 1927, p. 5. Reviewer: Garreta Busey.
*New York Post,* 7 August 1927. Reviewer: J. M. March.
*New York Times Book Review*, 21 August 1927, p. 5. Reviewer: Herbert S. Gorman.
*New York World*, 7 August 1927, p. 6m. Reviewer: Harry Salpeter.
*Opportunity* 5 (September 1927):270–271. Reviewer: E. Merrill Root.
*Pittsburgh Courier*, 27 August 1927, p. 11.
*Poetry* 31 (February 1928):284–286. Reviewer: Jessica Nelson North.
*St. Louis Post-Dispatch*, 17 August 1927.
*San Francisco Chronicle,* 7 August 1927.
*Springfield Massachusetts Republican*, 4 September 1927, p. 7f.
*Survey* 59 (1 November 1927):184. Reviewer: Gordon Lawrence.
*Washington Eagle*, 12 August 1927. Reviewer: Alice Dunbar Nelson.

*Wichita Beacon*, 15 January 1928.
*World Tomorrow* 10 (November 1927):472.
*Yale News Literary Supplement* 2, no. 1 (26 October 1927):4. Reviewer: W. D. Judson, Jr.

3. *Caroling Dusk.* Edited by Countée Cullen. New York: Harper & Brothers, 1927.
>"I have called this collection an anthology of verse by Negro poets rather than an anthology of Negro verse." (Foreword, p. xi.) This volume is noticeably bereft of verse in dialect, for as Cullen also noted in the Foreword: "It is enough to state that the day of dialect as far as Negro poets are concerned is in the decline." Therefore, the best poetry by Negro poets of the late nineteenth and early twentieth centuries is included in this comprehensive and enlightening anthology. The book also contains biographical sketches of the authors.

*Reviews*

*Asheville* (N.C.) *Citizen*, 1 January 1928.
*The Bookman* 67 (April 1928):203. Reviewer: Horace Gregory.
*Boston Transcript*, 12 December 1927.
*Charlotte Observer*, 1 January 1928.
*Chicago Bee*, 3 December 1929.
*Chicago News*, 23 November 1927.
*Cleveland Open Shelf*, December 1927, p. 133.
*Contemporary Verse* 23 (December 1927–January 1928):15. Reviewer: Benjamin Musser.
*Dallas News*, 5 February 1928. Reviewer: Clifton Blake.

*Detroit Free Press*, 27 November 1927. Reviewer: Amey Smyth.

*Detroit News*, 18 December 1927.

*Houston Post-Dispatch*, 6 November 1927.

*Louisville Courier-Journal*, 4 December 1927.

*Minneapolis Journal*, 20 November 1927.

*Nashville Banner*, 13 November 1927.

*New Haven Register*, 4 December 1927.

*New Republic* 53 (18 January 1928):25. Reviewer: Harry Alan Potamkin.

*New York Daily Worker*, 21 April 1928, p. 5. Reviewer: Lebarbe [pseud.].

*New York Evening Post*, 3 December 1927, p. 15. Reviewer: Laura Benet.

*New York Herald Tribune Books*, 27 November 1927, p. 21.

*New York News,* 31 December 1927. Reviewer: Mary White Ovington.

*Opportunity* 5 (December 1927):376. Reviewer: Gwendolyn B. Bennett.

*Philadelphia Public Ledger*, 10 December 1927.

*Portland Oregonian*, 12 February 1928.

*Springfield* (Ill.) *State Register*, 20 November 1927.

*Springfield* (Mass.) *Union*, 29 January 1928.

*Survey* 61 (October 1928):47. Reviewer, Guy B. Johnson.

*World Tomorrow* 11 (October 1928):423. Reviewer: De-Vere Allen.


4. *The Ballad of the Brown Girl: An Old Ballad Retold.*
New York: Harper & Brothers, 1927.
This is a retelling of an old story from the annals of English folklore—written in traditional quatrains for the most part. The story concerns the love of the "Brown Girl" for Lord Thomas, of

their marriage, and the ridicule of it by "Fair London" whom the lord had unwillingly rejected. Death comes to all three of the protagonists, bringing this old tale of racial prejudice and un-requited love to a swift and tragic end. A special edition of 500 copies was issued by *Opportunity* magazine.

*Reviews*

*Boston Transcript*, 5 May 1928, p. 5.
*Chicago Tribune*, 21 April 1928.
*New Haven Times Union*, 28 March 1928.
*New York American Hebrew*, 4 May 1928. Reviewer: Anne Kulique Kramer.
*New York Evening Post*, 7 July 1928, p. 8. Reviewer: A. K. Laing.
*New York Herald Tribune Books*, 6 May 1928, p. 21.
*New York Times Book Review*, 29 April 1928, p. 12. Reviewer: Percy Hutchison.
*St. Louis Post-Dispatch*, 28 March 1928.
*Salt Lake City Tribune,* 27 May 1928.
*San Francisco Chronicle*, 29 April 1928.
*Springfield Massachusetts Republican*, 17 October 1928, p. 8.
*Utica Press*, 19 May 1928.

5. *The Black Christ, And Other Poems.* New York: Harper & Brothers, 1929.
    The title poem is a modern story which leans heavily on the religious symbolism of the death and resurrection of Christ. The plot concerns the lynching of a Negro boy for a crime he did not, in reality, commit. The young boy appears to

his mother and brother, as if risen from the dead, like Christ; and thus, the title for the poem. The emotional intensity and devout attitude of the entire poem and the oftentimes stylized, self-conscious expressions tend to work against one another. This is considered one of Cullen's least successful poems. The other poems in the collection are, for the most part, brief lyrics on love and death.

*Reviews*

*Baltimore Afro-American*, 1 June 1929.

*Booklist* 26 (February 1930):195.

*Boston Transcript*, 31 December 1929, p. 2.

*Chicago Defender*, 9 November 1929. Reviewer: Dewey R. Jones.

*Christian Century* 47 (11 June 1930):757. Reviewer: Raymond Kresensky.

*Nation* 130 (12 March 1930):303–304. Reviewer: Granville Hicks.

*Nation and Athenaeum* (London) 46 (7 December 1929): 380 supplement. Reviewer: W. Palmer.

*New York Age*, 14 December 1929.

*New York Evening Post*, 14 December 1929, p. 13m. Reviewer: Vincent McHugh.

*New York Herald Tribune Books*, 2 February 1930.

*New York Telegram*, 30 November 1929.

*New York Times Book Review,* 1 December 1929, p. 7. Reviewer: Percy Hutchison.

*New York World*, 25 November 1929, p. 10m. Reviewer: Granville Hicks.

*Opportunity* 7 (March 1930):93. Reviewer: Clement Wood.

*Outlook* 153 (27 November 1929):509. Reviewer: Louise T. Nicholl.

*Poetry* 24 (February 1930):286–289. Reviewer: Bertha Ten Eyck James.

*Salt Lake City Tribune*, 27 May 1928.

*Southern Workman* 59 (February 1930):92. Reviewer: Edward Shillito.

*Times* (London) *Literary Supplement*, 21 November 1929, p. 948.

*Virginia Quarterly Review* 6 (January 1930):158. Reviewer: James Southall Wilson.

6. *The Medea, And Some Poems.* New York: Harper & Brothers, 1935.

> This rendition of *The Medea* of Euripides dispenses with verse form, except in the lines spoken by the choruses; yet there is some poetic rhythm apparent in much of the prose. Cullen has transferred the emotional power of this famous play into his quasi-poetic offering and—in spite of occasional lapses into mediocre phrasing—brings a modern freshness to this classical drama. The poems in the latter section include many sonnets and other short verses that follow the traditional romantic pattern of poetry Mr. Cullen admired.

*Reviews*

*Booklist* 32 (October 1935):37.

*Christian Science Monitor*, 4 September 1935, p. 12.

*Independent* 115 (November 1935):539.

*Nation* 141 (18 September 1935):336. Reviewer: Philip Blair Rice.

*New Republic* 85 (25 December 1935):207. Reviewer: Horace Gregory.
*New York Herald Tribune Books*, 15 September 1935, p. 17. Reviewer: Eda Lou Walton.
*New York Sun*, 20 September 1935, p. 28. Reviewer: P. M. Jack.
*New York Times Book Review*, 12 January 1936, p. 15. Reviewer: Peter Monro Jack.
*Opportunity* 13 (December 1935):381.

7. *The Lost Zoo* (*A Rhyme for the Young, But Not Too Young*), by Christopher Cat and Countée Cullen. New York: Harper & Brothers, 1940.
   This is a collection of charming little poems for people of all ages who enjoy humorous and touching verses about the animal world. The titles suggest the tenor of the book; "The Sleep-amitemore" and "The Snake-that-Walked-upon-His-Tail" are two examples of the characters who inhabit this book. A new edition was published by Follett in 1969.

*Reviews*

*New York Herald Tribune Books*, 8 December 1940, p. 16. Reviewer: Rosemary Benet.
*Saturday Review of Literature* 23 (16 November 1940):22. Reviewer: Katherine Scherman.

8. *On These I Stand: An Anthology of the Best Poems of Countée Cullen*. New York: Harper & Brothers, 1947.
   This book, posthumously published, contains

what the poet felt to be his best poems—"selected by himself and including six new poems never before published."

*Reviews*

*Atlantic Monthly* 179 (March 1947):144–145. Reviewer: John Ciardi.

*Booklist* 43 (1 March 1947):208.

*Bookmark* 8 (May 1947):9.

*Chicago Sun Book Week*, 9 March 1947, p. 5. Reviewer: A. J. Green.

*Cleveland Open Shelf*, May 1947, p. 10.

*Library Journal* 72 (15 February 1947):322. Reviewer: Gerald McDonald.

*New York Herald Tribune Books,* 31 August 1947, p. 4. Reviewer: Ruth Lechlitner.

*New York Times Book Review*, 23 February 1947, p. 26. Reviewer: Dudley Fitts.

*Opportunity* 25 (Summer 1947):170. Reviewer: William Stanley Braithwaite.

*PM*, 10 March 1947. Reviewer: Helen Wolfert.

*Poetry* 70 (July 1947):222–225. Reviewer: Harvey Curtis Webster.

*San Francisco Chronicle*, 27 July 1947, p. 14. Reviewer: George Snell.

*Saturday Review of Literature* 30 (22 March 1947):12. Reviewer: Arna Bontemps.

*United States Quarterly Book List* 3 (September 1947):242.

*Virginia Kirkus' Bookshop Service* 15 (1 January 1947):19.

*Wisconsin Library Bulletin* 43 (April 1947):64–66. Reviewer: Mary Katherine Reely.

*ARTICLES*

*General Articles*

9. "Countée Cullen in England." *Crisis* 36 (August 1929):270.
10. "Countée Cullen on French Courtesy." *Crisis* 36 (June 1929):193.
11. "Countée Cullen on Miscegenation." *Crisis* 36 (November 1929):373.
12. "Countée Cullen to His Friends." *Crisis* 36 (April 1929):119.
13. "The Creative Negro." In *America as Americans See It*, edited by Fred J. Ringel, p. 160. New York: Harcourt, Brace & Co., 1932.
14. "Development of Creative Expression." *High Points* 25 (September 1943):26–32.
15. "Elizabeth Prophet: Sculptress." *Opportunity* 8 (July 1930):204.
16. "The League of Youth." *Crisis* 26 (August 1923): 167–168. This is a copy of a speech delivered at Town Hall, New York, under the auspices of the League of Youth.

*"The Dark Tower" Series*

The following articles were written by Cullen when he was the assistant editor of *Opportunity*. This was a regular feature, always under "The Dark Tower" heading. A variety of subjects was included. However, any book reviews written for this feature are entered separately under the heading "Book Reviews." The entries below are listed chronologically.

17. "The Dark Tower." *Opportunity* 4 (December 1926): 388.
18. ————. *Opportunity* 5 (February 1927):53–54.
19. ————. *Opportunity* 5 (March 1927):86–87.
20. ————. *Opportunity* 5 (April 1927):118–119.
21. ————. *Opportunity* 5 (May 1927):149–150.
22. ————. *Opportunity* 5 (June 1927):180–181.
23. ————. *Opportunity* 5 (July 1927):210–211.
24. ————. *Opportunity* 5 (August 1927):240–241.
25. ————. *Opportunity* 5 (November 1927):336–337.
26. ————. *Opportunity* 5 (December 1927):373–374.
27. ————. *Opportunity* 6 (January 1928):20–21.
28. ————. *Opportunity* 6 (February 1928):52–53.
29. ————. *Opportunity* 6 (March 1928):90.
30. ————. *Opportunity* 6 (April 1928):120.
31. ————. *Opportunity* 6 (July 1928):210.
32. ————. *Opportunity* 6 (September 1928):271–273.

*Book Reviews*

33. Coyle, Kathleen. *It Is Better to Tell.* New York: E. P. Dutton, 1927. In *Opportunity* 6 (February 1928):52.
34. Heyward, Du Bose. *Porgy.* New York: George H. Doran, 1925. In *Opportunity* 3 (December 1925): 379.
35. Hughes, Langston. *The Weary Blues.* New York: Alfred A. Knopf, 1926. In *Opportunity* 4 (February 1926):73.

36. Johnson, James Weldon. *God's Trombones*. New York: Viking Press, 1927. In *The Bookman* 66 (October 1927):221–222.
37. Lowell, Amy. *Ballads for Sale*. Boston: Houghton Mifflin Co., 1924. In *Opportunity* 6 (February 1928):53.
38. ———. *Tendencies in Modern American Poetry*. New York: Macmillan Co., 1917. In *The Magpie* 20 (January 1921):31.
39. Root, E. Merrill. *Lost Eden*. New York: Unicorn Press, 1927. In *Opportunity* 6 (January 1928):20.
40. *The Spirit of St. Louis*. Edited by Arthur Hooley. New York: George H. Doran, 1927. In *Opportunity* 6 (February 1928):52.
41. Van Doren, Mark. *Spring Thunder and Other Poems*. New York: Thomas Seltzer, 1924. In *The Measure* (January 1925):15–17.

## POEMS IN PERIODICALS

42. "After a Visit." *Harvard Graduates' Magazine* 40 (December 1931):115.
43. "Any Human to Another." *This Quarter* 2 (December 1929):249–250.
44. "Apostrophe to the Land." *Phylon* 3 (Fourth Quarter):396–397.
45. "An Arista Ballade." *The Magpie* 21 (December 1921):7.
46. "At the Wailing Wall in Jerusalem." *New York Herald Tribune Books*, 6 March 1927, p. 4.

47. "Atlantic City Waiter." *New York Herald Tribune Books,* 23 August 1925.
48. "Ave Atque Vale." *The Magpie* 20 (January 1921): 99.
49. "The Ballad of the Brown Girl." *Palms* 2 (Early Summer 1924):19–26.
50. "La Belle, La Douce, La Grande." *New York Herald Tribune,* 10 July 1944.
51. "Black." *The Measure* (January 1925):4.
52. "Black Magdalens." *New York Herald Tribune Books,* 23 August 1925.
53. "Black Majesty." *Opportunity* 6 (May 1928):148.
54. "Blues Singer." *Folio* (N.Y.), 1923 [2]. This magazine is in the Schomburg Collection.
55. "Body and Soul." *Vanity Fair* 24 (June 1925):62.
56. "Bread and Wine." *Crisis* 26 (June 1923):64.
57. "Brown Boy to Brown Girl: Remembrance on a Hill." *Opportunity* 2 (September 1924):276.
58. "A Brown Girl Dead." *Survey Graphic* 6 (March 1925):661.
59. "The Changing Touch." *The Magpie* 20 (May 1921):6.
60. "Christmas: 1917. 1919." *The Magpie* 19 (December 1919):9.
61. "Christmas Thoughts." *The Magpie* 20 (December 1920):27.
62. "Clinton, Alma Mater, an Ode." *The Magpie* 21 (January 1922):38–39.
63. "Clinton to Her Graduates." *The Magpie* 20 (January 1921):44.
64. "Colored Blues Singer." *Palms* 2 (Early Fall 1924):83.
65. "Confession." *Opportunity* 4 (July 1926):209.
66. "Dad." *The Magpie* 21 (January 1922):91.

67. "The Dance of Love (After Reading René Maran's 'Batouala')." *Folio* (N.Y.), 1923 [2].
68. "Dream Time." *The Magpie* 20 (February 1921):42.
69. "Facultywocky." *The Magpie* 21 (November 1921): 33.
70. "The Fool Hath Said." *The Magpie* 19 (May 1920): 11.
71. "For a Cynic." *Harper's* 149 (December 1924):27.
72. "For a Fool." *Poetry* 26 (July 1925):204.
73. "For a Lady I Know." *Poetry* 24 (May 1924):77.
74. "For a Lovely Lady." *Harper's* 149 (December 1924): 27.
75. "For a Mouthy Woman." *Harper's* 150 (February 1925):342.
76. "For a Poet." *Harper's* 149 (December 1924):27.
77. "For a Preacher." *Poetry* 26 (July 1925):204.
78. "For a Singer." *Harper's* 149 (December 1924):27.
79. "For a Virgin Lady." *Poetry* 24 (May 1924):77.
80. "For a Wanton." *Poetry* 26 (July 1925):204.
81. "For Amy Lowell." *Poetry* 27 (January 1926):189.
82. "For an Atheist." *Harper's* 150 (February 1925):342.
83. "For an Evolutionist and His Opponent." *Harper's* 150 (February 1925):342.
84. "For John Keats, Apostle of Beauty." *Harper's* 150 (February 1925):342.
85. "For Joseph Conrad." *Harper's* 150 (February 1925): 342.
86. "For My Grandmother." *Poetry* 24 (May 1924):76.
87. "For Myself." *Harper's* 149 (December 1924):27.
88. "For One Who Gayly Sowed His Oats." *Poetry* 26 (July 1925):204.
89. "For Paul Lawrence Dunbar, Negro Laureat." *Harper's* 150 (February 1925):342.

90. "From Life to Love." *Opportunity* 3 (January 1925): 15.

91. "From the Dark Tower." *New York Herald Tribune*, 16 January 1924.

92. "Fruit of the Flower." *Harper's* 149 (November 1924): 754.

93. "Ghosts." *Tambour* (Paris) 1 (February 1929):10.

94. "The Greeting." *The Magpie* 21 (October 1921):7.

95. "Harlem Wine." *Survey* 53 (1 March 1925): 660.

96. "Heritage." *Survey* 53 (1 March 1925):674–675.

97. "Hunger." *The Measure* (January 1925):3.

98. "I Have a Rendezvous with Life." *The Magpie* 20 (January 1921):30.

99. "Icarian Wings." *The Clintonian*, June 1921, p. 78.

100. "If Love be Staunch." *Crisis* 30 (October 1925):280.

101. "If You Should Go." *Crisis* 24 (June 1922):85.

102. "In Memoriam." *Vanity Fair* 24 (June 1925):62.

103. "In Memory of Col. Charles Young." *Survey Graphic* 6 (March 1925):661.

104. "In Passing." *Palms* 2 (Early Fall 1924):84.

105. "In Praise of Boys." *New York Times*, 26 June 1922, p. 12.

106. "In Spite of Death." *Opportunity* 3 (July 1925):213.

107. "Incident." *World Tomorrow* 7 (March 1924):86.

108. "An Interlude." *New York National News*, 25 February 1932, p. 8.

109. "Judas Iscariot." *Southwestern Christian Advocate* 50 (15 March 1923):1.

   It is the revised version which appears in *Color*.

110. "Karenge Ya Marenge." *Opportunity* 20 (November 1942):323.

111. "King is Dead! Long Live the King!" *The Clintonian*, June 1921, p. 78.

112. "Lament." *Crisis* 30 (October 1925):280.
113. "Life." *The Magpie* 21 (January 1922):32.
114. "A Life of Dreams." *Southwestern Christian Advocate* 50 (1 February 1923):9.
115. "Lines to Certain of One's Elders." *Opportunity* 4 (June 1926):186.
116. "Litany of the Dark People." *The Student World,* October 1930, p. 330.
117. "Loss of Love." *Nation* 121 (1 July 1925):32.
118. "Lover in Ruins." *Opportunity* 4 (May 1926):157.
119. "Mary, Mother of Christ." *Crisis* 27 (March 1924): 222.
120. "Metamorphosis." *The Magpie* 20 (October 1920):13.
121. "Mood and Countermood." *Century* 119 (July 1929): 375.
122. "Near White." *Vanity Fair* 24 (June 1925):62.
123. "A Negro Mother's Lullaby (After a Visit to the Grave of John Brown)." *Opportunity* 20 (7 January 1942):7.
124. "Night Rain." *Crisis* 29 (February 1925):165.
125. "Nothing Endures." *Harpers* 158 (December 1926): 17.
126. "An Old Story." *The Carolina Magazine* 57 (May 1927):33.
127. "On Crushing a Caterpillar." *The Magpie* 21 (Christmas 1921):7.
128. "One Day We Played a Game." *Foot Prints* 1 (March 1927).
129. "Only the Polished Skeleton." *New York National News,* 14 April 1932, p. 8.
130. "Out of the Mouth of Babies (A Poem for a Precocious Child)." *New York National News,* 24 March 1932, p. 8.

131. "Pan on Boys' Week." *The Magpie* 20 (May 1921): 37.

132. "Parting." *The Magpie* 20 (October 1920):20.

133. "The Parting of the Ways." *The Magpie* 20 (February 1921):15.

134. "Poem." *New York National News,* 31 March 1932, p. 8.

135. "The Poet." *The Magpie* 20 (November 1920):25.

136. "Poet Puts His Heart to School." *Harper's* 154 (March 1927):412.

137. "A Prayer." *Southwestern Christian Advocate* 50 (4 January 1923):4.

138. "Protest." *Harper's* 154 (March 1927):412.

139. "Query." *The Magpie* 20 (November 1920):6.

140. "Questions and Answers." *The Magpie* 21 (January 1922):92.

141. "Red." *The Measure* (January 1925):4.

142. "Road Song." *Crisis* 24 (February 1923):160.

143. "Saturday's Child." *Century* 108 (September 1924): 713.

144. "Scandal and Gossip." *Vanity Fair* 24 (June 1925):62.

145. "Scottsboro, Too, Is Worth Its Song." *Los Angeles Post Dispatch*, 7 December 1934.

146. "She of the Dancing Feet Sings." *Survey Graphic* 6 (March 1925):661.

147. "The Shroud of Color." *American Mercury* 3 (November 1924):306–308.

148. "Simon the Cyrenian Speaks." *Poetry* 24 (May 1924): 76.

149. "Singing in the Rain." *Southwestern Christian Advocate* 50 (24 May 1923):8.

150. "The Simple Truth." *The Archive* 41 (October 1928):6.

151. "Snake-that-Walked-upon-His-Tail." *National Education Association Journal* 30 (December 1941): 258.

152. "A Song in Praise (To One Who Praised His Lady's Being Fair)." *Opportunity* 2 (September 1924): 275. Reprinted in *On These I Stand* as "A Song of Praise."

153. "Song in Spite of Myself." *Harper's* 158 (December 1928): 17.

154. "A Song of Bilitis." *New York National News*, 18 February 1932.

155. "A Song of Sour Grapes." *Palms* 4 (October 1926): 14.

156. "Song of the Poets." *The Magpie* 19 (March 1919): 34. Separate poems to Byron, Tennyson, Whittier, Longfellow, Dunbar, Poe, and "War Poets."

157. "Sonnet." *New York National News*, 7 April 1932, p. 8. Opening line: "I have not loved you in the noblest way."

158. "Sonnet." *New York National News*, 17 March 1932, p. 8. Opening line: "These are no wind-blown rumors . . ."

159. "Sonnet Dialogue." *New York National News*, 3 March 1932, p. 6.

160. "Sonnet to a Scornful Lady." *Opportunity* 4 (August 1926): 256.

161. "Sonnet to Her." *Crisis* 34 (March 1927): 13.

162. "The Spark." *The Measure* (January 1925): 31.

163. "Sweethearts." *Crisis* 27 (December 1923): 80.

164. "Tableau." *Survey Graphic* 6 (March 1925): 660.

165. "That Bright Chimeric Beast." *New Republic* 57 (23 January 1929): 267.

166. "A Thorn Forever in the Breast." *Opportunity* 5 (August 1927):225.
167. "Thoughts in a Zoo." *Crisis* 33 (December 1926):78.
168. "Three Hundred Years." *Crisis* 29 (April 1925):279.
169. "Three Nonsense Rhymes for My Three Goddaughters." *Scholastic* 27 (7 December 1935):8.
170. "Threnody for a Brown Girl." *Poetry* 26 (May 1925): 78–80.
171. "Timid Lover." *Folio* (N.Y.), 1923 [2].
172. "To a Brown Boy." *The Bookman* 58 (November 1923):245.
173. "To a Brown Girl." *Survey Graphic* 6 (March 1925): 660.
174. "To France." *Opportunity* 10 (August 1932):245.
175. "To John Haynes Holmes." *Crisis* 34 (March 1927): 13.
176. "To John Keats, Poet At Springtime." *Vanity Fair* 24 (June 1925):62.
177. "To Lovers of Earth: Fair Warning." *Harper's* 154 (February 1927):328.
178. "To One Who Said Me Nay." *Opportunity* 3 (May 1925):143.
179. "To the Swimmer." *Modern School* 5 (May 1918):142. This poem appeared under his former name of Countée Porter.
180. "The Touch." *Crisis* 26 (May 1923):22.
181. "Triolet." *The Magpie* 21 (Christmas 1921):27.
182. "Two Poets." *Opportunity* 7 (April 1929):109.
183. "Two Thoughts of Death." *Poetry* 29 (November 1926):75–76.
184. "Two Who Crossed a Line (He Crosses)." *World Tomorrow* 8 (November 1925):332.

185. "Two Who Crossed a Line (She Crosses)." *World Tomorrow* 8 (November 1925):332.
186. "Uncle Jim." *Opportunity* 3 (July 1925):213.
187. "The Unknown Color." *The Measure* (January 1925):4.
188. "Untitled Sonnet." *Trend* 1 (March–May 1932):9.
189. "Vagabond Yearnings." *The Magpie* 21 (January 1922):26.
190. "When I am Dead." *Opportunity* 1 (December 1923): 377.
191. "Who Knows?" *The Magpie* 19 (May 1919):4.
192. "Yet Do I Marvel." *Century* 109 (November 1924): 122.
193. "Youth Sings a Song of Rosebuds." *The Bookman* 60 (November 1924):285.
194. "Wind Bloweth Where it Listeth." *Poetry* 29 (November 1926):76–77.
195. "Wisdom Cometh with the Years." *Palms* 3 (Summer 1925):18.
196. "The Wise." *Nation* 119 (12 November 1924):522.
197. "Words to My Love." *Opportunity* 3 (July 1925): 213.


## MISCELLANEOUS WORKS

*Stories*

198. "The Frenchman's Bath." *The Magpie* 21 (November 1921):30–32.
199. "Invictus." *The Magpie* 21 (October 1921):22.

200. "Modernized Myths." *The Magpie* 21 (December 1921):15–17.

    The light, ironic touch and the technique of the surprise ending are attempted in these three early short-story efforts.

201. *My Lives and How I Lost Them*. New York: Harper & Brothers, 1942.

    When Christopher Cat convinces the author that "I am now in my *ninth* life," Cullen decides to help Christopher write down the account of his eight lives and how he lost them. Some charming, light stories, with occasional disdainful comments about the human being.

*Review*

*New York Herald Tribune Books*, 19 April 1942.

*Novel*

202. *One Way to Heaven*. New York: Harper & Brothers, 1932.

    The story of the people from two strata of society in Harlem. The plot centers mainly around Mattie, whose conversion to religion is hastened by her belief in Sam's conversion. He makes a racket of playing the revivals, but is touched by Mattie's faith in him. He marries her but cannot keep up the pretense of true belief. Their lives are contrasted with those of Mattie's employer, Constantia Brandon, and her group of Harlem "socialites."

*Reviews*

*Baltimore Afro-American*, 20 February 1932.

*Booklist* 28 (April 1932):349.

*Boston Evening Transcript*, 12 March 1932, p. 3.

*Louisiana Weekly*, 2 April 1932.

*New York Herald Tribune Books*, 28 February 1932, p. 3. Reviewer: Rudolf Fisher.

*New York National News*, 18 February 1932.

*New York Sun*, 19 February 1932. Reviewer: Robert Cantwell.

*New York Times Book Review*, 28 February 1932, p. 7. Reviewer: Elizabeth Brown.

*Norfolk Journal and Guide,* 30 April 1932. Reviewer: James G. Fleming.

*Philadelphia Tribune*, 17 March 1932.

*Pittsburgh Monthly Bulletin* 37 (May 1932):35.

*Saturday Review of Literature* 7 (12 March 1932):585. Reviewer: Martha Gruening.

*Southern Workman* 61 (March 1932):134–136. Reviewer: George A. Kuyper.

*Times* (London) *Literary Supplement*, 22 December 1932, p. 976.

*Wisconsin Library Bulletin* 28 (May 1932):163.


*Play*

203. Cullen, Countée, and Dodson, Owen. "The Third Fourth of July: A One-Act Play." *Theatre Arts* 30 (August 1946):488–493.

## Book Introduction

204. Cullen, Countée. Introduction to *The House of Vanity*, by Frank Ankenbrand and Benjamin Issac. Philadelphia: Leibman Press, 1928.

## Letter to the Editor

205. "Invocation." *PM*, 28 October 1943.
    Letter in which the poem "Hillburn the Fair" is featured.

## Spanish Civil War

206. *Writers Take Sides: Letters About the War in Spain from 418 American Authors*, p. 17. New York: League of American Writers, 1938.
    Cullen's statement: "I regard fascism as the supreme menace of our day, and I am against its every manifestation. I am unalterably for the people of Spain and for the legal Republican Government which they are striving so valiantly to maintain."

## Words to Music

207. "Christus Natus Est." Flushing (N.Y.): D. L. Schroeder, 1945.
    A song for mixed voices by Charles Marsh.
208. "Clinton My Clinton." *The Magpie* 21 (January 1922):14.

Music by W. Samuels, arranged by L. F. West.

209. "The Grim Troubadour, Op. 45." New York: Carl Fisher, 1927.

The music by Emerson Whithorne, using three poems by Cullen: "The Love Tree," "Lament," and "Hunger." The general title is derived from a line in "Lament."

210. "Seven Choruses from *The Medea* of Euripides." New York: Mercury Music Corp., 1942.

Music by Virgil Thomson—for women's voices.

211. "Tryst." New York: Circle Blue Print Co., n.d.

Music by Gene Bone and Howard Fenton—from the poem, "On Going."

212. "Saturday's Child." Boston: C. C. Birchard & Co., n.d.

Music by Emerson Whithorne—from the poems "Saturday's Child," "A Song of Praise," and "To One Who Said Me Nay."


## RECORDED WORKS

213. *An Anthology of Negro Poetry for Young People.* Folkways/Scholastic #7114.

Contents: For My Grandmother—Brown Boy and Girl—Under the Mistletoe—Red—The Unknown Color—For A Lady I Know—For a Poet.

214. *Anthology of Negro Poets.* Folkways/Scholastic #9791.

Contents: Heritage.

215. *Anthology of Negro Poets in the U.S.A.—200 Years.* Folkways/Scholastic #9792.

Contents: For a Poet—For a Lady I Know—Saturday's Children [*sic*]—Youth Sings a Song of Rosebuds.

216. *Sidney Poitier Reads Poetry of the Black Man, with Doris Belack.* United Artists #UAS-6693. Contents: Yet Do I Marvel.


## UNPUBLISHED WORKS

*Stories*

217. "The Adventures of Monkey Baboon." Cullen Private Collection.

This was written for children, to be illustrated by the Haitian artist Petion Savain. A few sketches are with the manuscript.

218. *The Little Zoo.* Cullen Private Collection.

A sequel to *The Lost Zoo.*

219. "You Learn to Love Them." Cullen Private Collection.

A projected book for children, of which only the chapter titles were written:

1. Introduction to them
2. Teachers' joy
3. Problem child
4. Scratch the worse we find some good
5. Lost, strayed or stolen
6. Prelude to examination
7. Portrait of colleagues
8. Teacher is absent
9. The things we teach them

10. Charlie
11. They create
12. Soldiers
13. Graduation day
14. Pockets out

*Play*

220. Cullen, Countée, and Bontemps, Arna. "St. Louis Woman." Cullen Private Collection.

The following are reviews of the musical production of "St. Louis Woman," presented at the Martin Beck Theatre on 30 March 1946.

*Reviews*

*Catholic World* 163 (May 1946):170. Reviewer: Euphemia Van Rensselaer Wyatt.
*Commonweal* 43 (19 April 1946):14.
*Life* 20 (29 April 1946):63–64.
*New York Times*, 1 April 1946, p. 22. Reviewer: Lewis Nichols.
*Newsweek* 27 (15 April 1946):84.
*Time* 47 (8 April 1946):47.

221. "The Spirit of Peace." Cullen Private Collection.
   A typewritten manuscript of a play written for the ninth grade at P.S. 139, New York City, where Cullen taught.

*Verse*

222. "The Freedom Song." Cullen Private Collection.

      This was to be one of the verses set to music which Cullen wanted to use for a series of radio programs. His plans were not completed before his death.

223. "Poem for a Little Child." Beinecke Library, Yale University.

      The poet noted on the manuscript that the poem was written in 1931.

224. "To W. E. B. DuBois." Beinecke Library, Yale University.

      Printed in a menu-program for a gathering of persons in honor of Dr. DuBois, Cafe Savarin, 13 April 1924.

# 5

# *Writings*
# *About Cullen*

THIS chapter contains material written about Cullen in newspapers and in parts of books, including unpublished manuscripts. Obituary notices and tributes to the poet are at the conclusion of the chapter. All entries are arranged alphabetically by author or by title under the various headings. A few annotations are given in order to clarify some entries. Pages cited are for information about Cullen only and do not always indicate complete pagination for the text.

## ARTICLES

225. Allison, Madeline, ed. "The Horizon." *Crisis* 23 (March 1922):219.
     This covers many of Cullen's activities at high school.
226. ———. "The Horizon." *Crisis* 24 (October 1922):272.

This summarizes Cullen's awards and activities up to the time of his first year in college.

227. "Art and the Negro." *Springfield* (Ill.) *Register*, 10 December 1925.

228. Baldwin, James. "Rendezvous with Life: An Interview with Countée Cullen." *The Magpie* 26 (Winter 1942):19–21.

229. "Baltimore Hotel Bars Countée Cullen." *New York News*, 8 May 1926.

230. Bland, Edward. "Racial Bias and Negro Poetry." *Poetry* 63 (March 1944):328–329.

231. Bontemps, Arna. "Countée Cullen; American Poet." *New York Peoples Voices*, 26 January 1946, pp. S2–S3.

232. "Book Studio Group Honors Cullen, Poet." *New York Amsterdam News*, 17 September 1930, p. 10.

233. *The Bookman* 62 (February 1926):747.
Brief remark about Cullen's age and the fact that he was attending Harvard. Part of a feature called "The Gossip Shop."

234. Brawley, Benjamin. "The Negro Literary Renaissance." *Southern Workman* 56 (April 1927): 181–182.

235. "Bride of Negro Poet in Church Ceremony Here Yesterday." *New York World*, 10 April 1928. Photograph of Yolande DuBois Cullen.

236. Brown, Evelyn S. "Distinguished Achievement Recognized." *Southern Workman* 56 (February 1927):85.

237. Calverton, V. F. "The Negro's New Belligerent Attitude." *Current History* 30 (September 1929): 1084.

238. Calvin, Floyd J. "Countée Cullen Tells How He Writes." *Pittsburgh Courier,* 18 June 1927, sec. 2, p. 4.

239. Chamberlain, John. "The Negro as Writer." *The Bookman* 70 (February 1930):609–610.

240. Clark, Margaret. "Overtones in Negro Poetry." *Interracial Review* 9 (July 1936):106.

241. ———. "The Voice of a Race." *Interracial Review* 9 (April 1936):58.

242. "Conclude Literary Shop Talk Tonight." *Springfield* (Mass.) *Union,* 8 May 1928.

243. "Countée Cullen." *American Peoples Encyclopedia.* 1953 ed. vol. 6, p. 604.

244. "Countée Cullen." *Chicago Bee,* 24 December 1927.

245. "Countée Cullen." *Encyclopedia Americana.* 1957 ed. Vol. 8, p. 295.

246. "Countée Cullen." *Springfield* (Mass.) *Union,* 27 December 1927.

247. "Countée Cullen Divorced." *New York Times,* 28 March 1930, p. 22.

248. "Countée Cullen Given Degree by Harvard U." *Chicago Bee,* 10 July 1926.

249. "Countée Cullen Gives Readings." *Cleveland Plain Dealer,* 28 April 1926.

250. "Countée Cullen Has Another Birthday." *Baltimore Afro-American,* 25 May 1929.

251. "Countée Cullen Lectures at Brown University to 800 Poetry Lovers." *Pittsburgh Courier,* 19 December 1931, p. 3.

252. "Countée Cullen, Negro Poet, To Wed Baltimorean." *Baltimore Sun,* 26 March 1928.

253. "Countée Cullen Plans Anthology." *New York Amsterdam News,* 17 November 1926.

254. "Countée Cullen Poet by Accident." *Baltimore Afro-American*, 29 March 1930.

255. "Countée Cullen to Read." *Chicago Post*, 24 December 1925.

256. "Countée Cullen Weds Daughter of Dr. DuBois." *New York Herald Tribune*, 10 April 1928.

257. "Countée P. Cullen—Who Is He?" *Pittsburgh Courier*, 14 November 1925, sec. 2, p. 9.

258. "Cullen Carries Off Witter Bynner Prize." *New York University Daily News*, 8 December 1925.

259. "Cullen-DuBois Nuptials." *Tattler*, 13 April 1928. Article is in Cullen vertical file, Beinecke Library, Yale University.

260. "Cullen, Noted Poet of Harlem, Marries." *New York News*, 10 April 1928.

261. "Cullen Praises Waterbury Work for the Negroes." *Waterbury Republican*, 27 November 1928.

262. "Cullen Supports Communists!" *The* (n.p.) *Union*, 22 September 1932.
    Although one handwritten source states Springfield, Mass., the newspaper has not been able to verify this citation. The vertical file on Cullen in the Schomburg Collection has this article, but place of origin is not indicated on their copy.

263. "Cullen to Edit Mexican Magazine." *New York Amsterdam News*, 5 May 1926, p. 16.

264. "Cullen Weds Ida Roberson." *New York Amsterdam News*, 5 October 1940.

265. "Cullen Wins Poetry Prize." *New York Times*, 9 December 1925, p. 20.

266. "Cullen's Lecture on Negro Poets Enjoyed by Many."

*Providence* (R.I.) *News Tribune*, 1 December 1931.

267. Davis, Arthur P. "The Alien-and-Exile Theme in Countée Cullen's Racial Poems." *Phylon* 14 (Fourth Quarter 1953):390–400.

268. Dismond, Geraldyn. "Through the Lorgnette: Countée Cullen." *Pittsburgh Courier*, 28 May 1927, sec. 2, p. 1.

269. DuBois, W. E. B. "So the Girl Marries." *Crisis* 35 (June 1928):192–193.

270. Emerson, Dorothy, ed. "The Poetry Corner." *Scholastic* 27 (7 December 1935):8.

271. "Entertain Colored Poet." *Chicago Daily Journal,* 29 December 1925.

272. "The First Reader." *New York World*, 7 January 1925.
    Concerns Cullen's winning a prize for "The Shroud of Color."

273. "Fractional Tones Figure in League's Concert." *New York Herald Tribune*, 21 February 1926.
    Concerns Emerson Whithorne's arrangement of "Saturday's Child."

274. Gallant [pseud.?] "Members of the Arts and Society Honor Noted Poet." *New York National News*, 10 March 1932, p. 6.

275. "Guggenheim Fund Makes 75 Awards." *New York Times*, 19 March 1928, p. 8.

276. "Harlem's Negro Poet to Read Verse Here." *Milwaukee Journal*, 6 December, sec. 2, n.p.

277. "Harper & Brothers Publish Countée Cullen's 'Color.'" *New York Amsterdam News*, 18 November 1925, sec. 2, p. 16.

278. "Harvard Negro Poet Wins Another Prize." *Christian Science Monitor*, 10 November 1925.

279. "Harvard Negro Pupil Wins Poetry Prize." *Boston Herald*, 12 October 1925.

280. "The Horizon." *Crisis* 31 (December 1925):83. Notice of Cullen's receipt of the John Reed Memorial Poetry Prize.

281. ———. *Crisis* 31 (February 1926):179. A notice of Cullen's receipt of the Witter Bynner undergraduate poetry prize for 1925.

282. ———. *Crisis* 33 (February 1927):206 A photograph of Cullen and news of prizes awarded him. Also, information about his education and *Color*.

283. Horne, Frank S. "Black Verse." *Opportunity* 2 (November 1924):330–332.

284. "In the Vanguard." *New York Amsterdam News*, 2 February 1935, p. 9.

285. "Introducing Countée Cullen." *Macon* (Ga.) *Telegraph*, 10 March 1926.

286. Kerlin, Robert T. "Conquest by Poetry." *Southern Workman* 56 (June 1927):283–284.

287. ———. "A Pair of Youthful Negro Poets." *Southern Workman* 53 (April 1924):178–181. An introduction to some poetry by Cullen and Langston Hughes.

288. Knox, Winifred. "American Negro Poetry." *The Bookman* (London) 81 (October 1931):16–17.

289. Lash, John S. "The Anthologist and the Negro Author." *Phylon* 8 (First Quarter 1947):68–76.

290. "Line o' Type or Two." *Chicago Daily Tribune*, 6 July [1926].

291. *The Light* 3 (24 September 1927):12.
292. McCormack, Margaret. "Countée Cullen." *Interracial Review* 12 (May 1939):74.
293. "Milestones: Countée Cullen, Poet." *Philadelphia Tribune*, 21 May 1936.
294. "N.Y.U. Negro Student Again Scores as Poet." *New York World*, 1 October 1924.
295. *Nation* 126 (28 March 1928):335.
296. "Negro Poet Again Honored." *Boise Statesman*, 20 December 1925.
297. "A Negro Poet and the White North Carolianians." *New York Age*, n.d. Countée Cullen vertical file sheet #19, Schomburg Collection.
298. "Negro Poet Answers Restaurant Rebuff." *Buffalo Evening News*, 17 November 1930, p. 1.
299. "Negro Poet in Detroit to Present Reading." *Detroit News,* 11 December 1927.
300. "Negro Poet Married." *New York Times*, 10 April 1928, p. 31.
301. "Negro Poets, Singers in the Dawn." *Negro History Bulletin* 2 (November 1938):9.
302. "Negro Renaissance." *New York Herald Tribune*, 7 May 1925, p. 16.
303. "Negro Student Wins Phi Beta Kappa Honor." *New York Times*, 20 March 1925, p. 19.
304. "The Negro Wins." *Southwestern Christian Advocate* 50 (13 November 1923):2.
305. "Negro Wins Poetry Prize." *New York Herald Tribune*, 9 December 1925.
306. "Negro Wins Prize in Poetry Contest." *New York Times*, 2 December 1923, sec. 2, p. 1.

307. "Negro Worker Wins Harmon Art Prizes." *New York Times*, 2 January 1927, p. 15.

308. *New York Evening World*, 1 June 1925.

A letter from Clement Wood concerning Cullen and Langston Hughes wherein Wood justifies the choice of the *Opportunity* poetry contest judges who gave Hughes the First Prize. *See also* "Prize Poem—A Silly Jingle."

309. *Opportunity* 3 (May 1925):159.

A notice in the regular feature "Social Progress" of Cullen's election to Phi Beta Kappa. Other details of his life are also cited.

310. ———— 3 (December 1925):387.

Information in "Social Progress" column about Cullen winning first prize in the Witter Bynner contest.

311. ———— 4 (June 1926):185.

Comments about "Yet Do I Marvel."

312. ———— 6 (August 1928):249.

A note concerning Cullen's departure for Europe in the regular feature "Survey of the Month."

313. ———— 12 (July 1934):221.

A notice in "Survey of the Month" concerning Cullen's appointment as head of the English Department, Dillard University—a position he finally did not accept.

314. "Out for Communists." *Baltimore Afro-American*, 24 September 1932.

315. Oxley, Lloyd G. "The Black Man in World Literature." *Philadelphia Tribune*, 27 May 1937.

316. ————. "The Negro in the World's Literature." *New York Amsterdam News*, 30 May 1928, p. 16. These last two entries are identical in text.

317. *Pittsburgh Courier*, 28 March 1925.
     About Cullen's election to Phi Beta Kappa.
318. "Poet to Read Own Work." *Washington Evening Star*, 16 March 1928.
319. Postles, Grace V. "Literary Echoes: Countée Cullen." n.p., n.d.
     Countée Cullen vertical file sheet #10, Schomburg Collection.
320. "Prize Poem—A Silly Jingle." *Boston Chronicle*, 30 May 1925, p. 1.
     A reprint of a letter by Eugene Gordon in which he calls Hughes's "The Weary Blues" a "silly jingle." Gordon objected to Hughes receiving the first prize in the *Opportunity* contest. *See also* entry #308.
321. "Prize to American Poet." *New York World*, 19 October 1925, p. 2.
322. Reid, William Watkins. "Countée Cullen." *The Advocate*, 3 June 1926, pp. 11–12.
323. Reimherr, Beulah. "Race Consciousness in Countée Cullen's Poetry." *Susquehanna University Studies* 7 (1963):65–82.
324. Reiss, Winold. "Countée Cullen." *Survey* 54 (1 June 1925):299.
     A color portrait of Cullen.
325. Richards, William C. "That's How They Told It To Me." *Detroit Free Press*, 13 November 1927.
326. Robb, Izetta Winter. "From the Darker Side." *Opportunity* 4 (December 1926):381–382.
327. Rothermel, Winifred. "Countée Cullen Sees Future for Race." *Birmingham News*, 29 January 1928.
     This same article appeared in the *St. Louis Argus*, 3 February 1928.

328. *St. Louis Post-Dispatch*, 13 November 1927.
     A white reader's reaction to *Caroling Dusk*.
329. *Salt Lake City Tribune*, 27 December 1925.
     William Allen White's opinion of Cullen. *See also* entry #349.
330. Shillito, Edward. "Poet and the Race Problem." *Century* 46 (17 July 1929):915–916.
331. Smith, Robert A. "The Poetry of Countée Cullen." *Phylon* 11 (Third Quarter 1950):216–221.
332. "Somehow Smelly." *Baltimore Evening Sun*, 26 April 1926, sec. 2, p. 19.
     Editorial about Emerson Hotel's refusal to let Cullen speak there.
333. "Soprano and Negro Poet Give Program." *Milwaukee Journal* [31 December 1925].
334. Stribling, T. J. "Noted Southern Writer Discovers Real Harlem." *New York World*, 11 March 1928, p. 7M.
335. "Surrounded by His Books, Countée Cullen is Happy." *Christian Science Monitor*, 23 October 1925, p. 6.
336. Taussig, Charlotte E. "The New Negro as Revealed in His Poetry." *Opportunity* 5 (April 1927):111.
337. Van Doren, Carl. "The Younger Generation of Negro Writers." *Opportunity* 2 (May 1924):144–145.
338. Walton, Lester A. "Protests Holding Negro Artists to Racial Themes." *New York World*, 15 May 1927, p. 16M.
339. Ward, Edith, ed. "Poetry Corner." *Scholastic* 36 (12 February 1940):25.
340. Wells, Henry W. "Old Wine into Old Bottles." *Voices, A Quarterly of Poetry*, Spring 1947.
341. *Who's Who in America*. 1930–1931 ed., vol. 16, pp. 616–617.

342. ———. 1932–1933 ed., vol. 17, p. 631.

343. ———. 1934–1935 ed., vol. 18, p. 646.

344. ———. 1936–1937 ed., vol. 19, pp. 653–654.

345. *Who's Who in Colored America.* 1927 ed., p. 49.

346. ———. 1928–1929 ed., p. 93.

347. ———. 1933–1937 ed., p. 138.

348. ———. 1938–1940 ed., p. 140.

349. "William Allen White's Latest Enthusiasm." *Dallas Herald*, 8 January 1926.

350. Woodruff, Bertram L. "The Poetic Philosophy of Countée Cullen." *Phylon* 1 (Third Quarter 1940): 213–223.

351. "Young Cullen is on Staff of 'Opportunity.'" *Pittsburgh Courier*, 30 October 1926.

352. "A Young Negro Poet." *Kansas City Star*, 8 May 1926.

353. "Young Negro Poet Guest of Woman's Club." *Chicago Daily Journal*, 28 December 1925.

354. "Young Negro Poet to Talk Here Sunday." *St. Paul Dispatch*, 3 February 1928.

355. "Youthful Creative Effort Wins Reward." *Salt Lake City Tribune*, 15 April 1928.

## PUBLISHED BIOGRAPHY

356. Ferguson, Blanche E. *Countée Cullen and the Negro Renaissance.* New York: Dodd, Mead, 1966.

## PARTS OF BOOKS

357. Blankenship, Russell. *American Literature As An Expression of the National Mind*. New York: Henry Holt, 1949.
358. Bone, Robert. *The Negro Novel in America*. New Haven: Yale University Press, 1958.
359. Brawley, Benjamin. *The Negro Genius*. New York: Dodd, Mead, 1937.
360. ———. *The Negro in Literature and Art*. New York: Duffield, 1918.
361. Brown, Sterling. *Negro Poetry and Drama*. Washington: Associates in Negro Folk Education, 1937.
362. Bronz, Stephen H. *Roots of Negro Racial Consciousness*. New York: Libra, 1964.
363. Bullock, Ralph W. *In Spite of Handicaps*. New York: Association Press, 1927.
364. Butcher, Margaret Just. *The Negro in American Culture*. New York: Alfred A. Knopf, 1956.
365. Dancy, John. *Sand Against the Wind*. Detroit: Wayne State University Press, 1966.
   The account of Cullen in pp. 124–127 tells the surprising story of Dancy's first view of the young Cullen as an offender in Juvenile Court. The author is now dead. Some of the facts are definitely incorrect; but the recorder for Dancy feels that the nature of this first encounter between the man and the boy is basically true.
366. Dowd, Jerome. *The Negro in American Life*. New York: Century, 1926.
367. DuBois, William Edward Burghardt. *The Autobio-*

*graphy of W. E. B. DuBois.* New York: International Publishing Co., Inc., 1968.

There is no mention of Cullen in the text, but two photographs between pages 192 and 193 are interesting: that of the Cullen–DuBois wedding party and one of the bride, Yolande DuBois.

368. Fauset, Arthur Huff. *For Freedom: A Biographical Story of the American Negro.* Philadelphia: Franklin Publishing & Supply, 1927.

369. Fletcher, Martin, ed. *Our Great Americans.* Chicago: Gamma Corp., 1953.

370. Ford, Nick Aaron. *The Contemporary Negro Novel: A Study in Race Relations.* College Park, Md.: McGrath Publishing Co., 1968 c1936.

Of limited value for the Cullen scholar.

371. Green, Elizabeth Lay. *The Negro in Contemporary American Literature.* College Park, Md.: McGrath Pub. Co., 1968 c1928.

372. Gregory, H., and Zaturenska, M. *History of American Poetry, 1900–1940.* New York: Harcourt, Brace & Co., 1946.

373. Gross, Seymour, and Hardy, John Edward, eds. *Images of the Negro in American Literature.* Chicago: University of Chicago Press, 1966.

374. Herzberg, Max J., ed. *The Reader's Encyclopedia of American Literature.* New York: Thomas Y. Crowell, 1962.

375. Hughes, Langston, and Meltzer, Milton. *A Pictorial History of the Negro in America.* New York: Crown Publishers, Inc., 1956.

376. Issac, Edith J. R. *The Negro in the American Theatre.* New York: Theatre Arts, 1947.

377. Johnson, James Weldon. *Black Manhattan.* New York: Alfred A. Knopf, 1930.

378. Kreymborg, Alfred. *A History of American Poetry.* New York: Tudor, 1934.

379. ———. *Our Singing Strength.* New York: Tudor, 1941.

380. Locke, Alain. "The Negro in American Literature." In *New World Writing.* New York: New World Press, 1952.

381. Loggins, Vernon. *The Negro Author.* New York: Columbia University Press, 1931.

382. Margolies, Edward. *Native Sons: A Critical Study of Twentieth-Century Negro American Authors.* Philadelphia: J. B. Lippincott, 1968.

383. Mays, Benjamin. *The Negro's God as Reflected in His Literature.* Boston: Chapman & Grimes, 1938.

384. Millett, Fred B. *Contemporary American Authors.* New York: Harcourt, Brace & Co., 1940.

385. Mims, Edwin. *Christ of the Poets.* New York, Nashville: Abingdon-Cokesbury, 1948.

386. Murray, Florence, ed. *The Negro Handbook.* New York: Macmillan Co., 1949.

387. Nyren, Dorothy, ed. *A Library of Literary Criticism.* New York: Ungar, 1960.

388. Ploski, Harry A., and Brown, Roscoe C., Jr., eds. *The Negro Almanac.* New York: Bellwether Publishing Co., 1967.
Baltimore is given as Cullen's place of birth.

389. Redding, J. Saunders. *To Make a Poet Black.* Chapel Hill: University of North Carolina Press, 1939.

390. Survey Graphic. *Harlem, Mecca of the New Negro.* New York: Survey Graphic, 1925.

391. Wagner, Jean. *Les Poètes Nègres des Etats-Unis*. Paris: Librairie Istra, 1963.
392. Witham, W. Tasker. *Panorama of American Literature*. New York: Stephen Daye Press, 1947.

## MISCELLANEOUS WRITINGS

393. "Afro-Arts Sponsors C. Cullen Memorial." *New York Amsterdam News*, 1 April 1950.
394. "Cullen Memorial." *New York Sun*, 16 January 1946.
395. Jackson, Walter Van. "The Countée Cullen Memorial Collection at Atlanta University." *Crisis* 54 (May 1947):140–142.
396. Porter, Dorothy B. *North American Negro Poets: A Bibliographical Checklist of Their Writings, 1760–1944*. Hattiesburg, Miss.: Book Farm, 1945.

## UNPUBLISHED WRITINGS

397. Dinger, Helen Josephine. "A Study of Countée Cullen." Master's thesis, Columbia University, 1953.
398. Jerome, Fred. "Langston Hughes and Countée Cullen: Forces in New Negro Poetry." Honors thesis, The City College New York, January 1960.
399. Johnson, Charles S. "Countée Cullen Was My Friend." This speech was delivered at the ceremony which renamed the 136th Street Branch of the New York Public Library the Countée Cullen Branch—12 September 1951. Schomburg Collection.
400. ———. "Source Material For Patterns of Negro Segre-

gation, New York City." Carnegie–Myrdal Study, n.d. Mimeographed.

The interview with Cullen, listed here, took place on 28 September 1939. Schomburg Collection.

′ 401. Reimherr, Beulah. "Countée Cullen: A Biographical and Critical Study." Master's thesis, University of Maryland, 1960.

A study which investigates religion and atavism in Cullen's work. There is also a lengthy discussion of the confusion surrounding his birth.

## OBITUARIES AND TRIBUTES

402. Benet, William Rose. "Phoenix Nest." *Saturday Review of Literature* 29 (23 February 1946):44.

403. Bontemps, Arna. "Countée Cullen." *Film News*, January 1946.

404. Burstein, Joel. "Countée Cullen, Famous Grad, Poet and Author, Passes Away." *Clinton* [High School] *News*, 18 January 1946.

405. *Chicago Defender*, 26 January 1946.

Written by W. E. B. DuBois.

406. "Countée Cullen, Negro Poet, Dead." *New York Times*, 10 January 1946, p. 23.

407. "Countée Cullen, Negro Poet, Dies." *New York Daily Worker*, 10 January 1946, p. 8.

408. "Countée Cullen, Negro Poet, Dies." *New York Sun*, 10 January 1946.

409. "Countée Cullen, Negro Poet, Is Dead." *New York Post*, 10 January 1946.

410. "Countée Cullen, Noted Poet, Taken By Death."

*New York Amsterdam News*, 12 January 1946, p. 1.

411. "Countée Cullen, One of Great U. S. Poets, Dies." *Chicago Defender*, 12 January 1946.

412. *Current Biography* 7 (March 1946):20.

413. Dodson, Owen. "Countée Cullen." *Phylon* 7 (January–March 1946):19–20.

414. "Facts of Cullen's Life Few, Direct and Simple." *New York Amsterdam News*, 19 January 1946, p. 2.

415. Hughes, Langston. "Here to Yonder: Countée Cullen." *Chicago Defender*, 2 February 1946.

416. *Los Angeles Sentinal*, 17 January 1946.

417. Maleska, Eugene T. "Countée Cullen—1903–1946." *Embers* 4 (May–June 1946):14–15.

418. *New York Villager*, 17 January 1946.

419. *Newsweek*, 21 January 1946, p. 79.

420. *Opportunity* 24 (April–June 1946):90.

421. "The Passing of a Poet." *Negro History Bulletin* 9 (February 1946):98.

422. *Poetry* 68 (April 1946):58–59.

423. *Publishers' Weekly* 149 (26 January 1946):628.

424. Smallwood, Will. "Tribute to Countée Cullen." *Opportunity* 25 (Summer 1947):168–169.

425. "A Star Falls." *Headlines and Pictures* 2 (February 1946):12–14.

   An interesting but inaccurate description of Cullen's early life.

426. "3000 at Funeral of Countée Cullen." *New York Times*, 13 January 1946, p. 44.

427. *Time*, 21 January 1946, p. 62.

428. *Wilson Library Bulletin* 20 (March 1946):456.

# 6

## Newspaper References

THE twenty-three entries in this chapter are untitled newspaper references to different activities of Countée Cullen, gathered from clippings in his widow's possession. Only the title of the periodical and the date are given.

429. *Baltimore Sun*, 11 May 1926.
430. *Birmingham Herald*, 6 December 1925.
431. *Boston Evening Transcript*, 24 July 1926.
432. *Boston Guardian*, 29 October 1927.
433. *Boston Herald*, 10 December 1927.
434. ———, 3 March 1928.
435. ———, 5 May 1928.
436. *Brooklyn Life*, 16 January 1926.
437. *Buffalo Evening Times*, 10 March 1928.
438. *Chicago Defender*, 9 November 1929.
439. *Dallas News*, 20 December 1926.

440. *Detroit News,* 11 December 1927.
441. *Harvard Crimson,* 21 October 1925.
442. *London Daily News,* 23 December 1927.
443. *Louisiana Weekly Bookchat,* 2 April 1932.
444. *New York Daily Worker,* 6 October 1941.
445. *New York Herald Tribune,* 7 May 1925.
446. ————, 24 January 1926.
447. ————, 1 April 1928.
448. *New York World,* 21 March 1928.
449. *St. Louis Globe Democrat,* 16 January 1926.
450. *South Bend Tribune,* 25 December 1927.
451. *Trenton Times Advertiser,* 18 September 1927.

# 7

## Poetry Anthologies

THIS chapter contains anthologies of poetry in which the poems of Countée Cullen appear. The listing cannot pretend to be absolutely definitive, but a broad coverage has been made—including a few foreign language titles. The arrangement is alphabetical by compiler, or by title, if no editor is given.

452. Adams, Franklin P., ed. *The Conning Tower Book.* New York: Macy-Masius, 1926.
453. Ballagas, Emilio. *Mapa de la Poesia Negra Americana.* Buenos Aires: Editorial Pleamar [1946].
454. Berti, Luigi, ed. *Canti Negri (Negro Songs).* Florence: Fussi, 1949.
455. *Black and Unknown Bards: A Collection of Negro Poetry.* n.p., Kent County, England: Aldington, 1958.
456. Blair, Walter, ed. *The United States in Literature.* Chicago: Scott, Foresman & Co., 1963.

457. Blum, David L., ed. *Some Recent New York University Verse*. New York: New York University Press, 1926.

458. Bontemps, Arna, ed. *Golden Slippers: An Anthology of Negro Poetry for Young Readers*. New York: Harper & Brothers, 1941.

459. ————. *Hold Fast to Dreams*. Chicago: Follett, 1969.

460. Braithwaite, William Stanley, ed. *Anthology of Magazine Verse for 1925, and Yearbook of American Poetry*. Boston: Brimmer, 1925.

461. ————. *Anthology of Magazine Verse for 1926, and Yearbook of American Poetry*. Boston: Brimmer, 1926.

462. ————. *Anthology of Magazine Verse for 1927, and Yearbook of American Poetry*. Boston: Brimmer, 1927.

463. Brown, Sharon, ed. *Poetry of Our Time*. Chicago: Scott, Foresman, 1928.

464. Brown, Sterling, and others, eds. *The Negro Caravan*. New York: Dryden Press, 1941.

465. Bryant, William Cullen, ed. *Library of Poetry and Song*. Vol. 1. Rev. and enlg. ed. New York: Doubleday, Doran, 1925.

466. Calverton, V. F., ed. *Anthology of American Negro Literature*. New York: Modern Library, 1929.

467. Clark, Thomas Curtis, ed. *One Thousand Quotable Poems*. Chicago: Willett, Clark, 1937.

468. ————. *Poems of Justice*. Chicago: Willett, Clark, 1929.

469. Clark, Thomas, and Gillespie, Esther A., eds. *Quotable Poems*. Vol. 1. Chicago: Willett, Clark, 1928.

470. ————. *Quotable Poems*. Vol. 2. Chicago: Willett, Clark, 1931.

471. Connell, Catherine, ed. *Love Poems, Old and New.* New York: Random House, 1943.

472. Cooper, Alice Cecilia, ed. *Poems of Today.* New York: Ginn & Co., 1939.

473. Cromwell, Otelia, and others, eds. *Readings from Negro Authors.* New York: Harcourt, Brace & Co., 1931.

474. Doud, Margery, and Parsley, Cleo M., eds. *Father: An Anthology of Verse.* New York: Dutton, 1931.

475. Dreer, Herman, ed. *American Literature by Negro Authors.* New York: Macmillan Co., 1950.

476. Drinkwater, John, and others, eds. *Twentieth-Century Poetry.* Boston: Houghton Mifflin Co., 1929.

477. Eleazer, Robert B., ed. *Singers in the Dawn.* Atlanta: Conference on Education and Race Relations, 1934, 1935.

478. Ellsworth, William Webster, ed. *Readings from the New Poets.* New York: Macmillan Co., 1928.

479. Fish, Helen Dean, ed., *The Boy's Book of Verse.* Philadelphia: J. B. Lippincott, 1951.

480. Flower, Margaret, and Flower, Desmond, eds. *Cassell's Anthology of English Poetry.* 2d ed. New York: Cassell & Co., 1946.

481. *Four Negro Poets: Claude McKay, Jean Toomer, Countée Cullen, Langston Hughes.* Introduction by Alain Locke. New York: Simon & Shuster [1927].

482. Gillis, Adolph, and Benet, William Rose, eds. *Poems for Modern Youth.* Boston: Houghton Mifflin Co., 1938.

483. Giniger, Kenneth Seaman, ed. *America, America, America.* New York: F. Watts, 1957.

484. Hollowell, Lillian, ed. *A Book of Children's Literature.* New York: Rinehart, 1950.

485. Hughes, Langston, and Bontemps, Arna, eds. *The Poetry of the Negro.* New York: Doubleday, 1949.

486. Johnson, Charles, ed. *Ebony and Topaz: A Collectanea.* New York: *Opportunity*, 1927.

487. Johnson, James Weldon, ed. *The Book of American Negro Poetry.* New York: Harcourt, Brace & Co., 1931.

488. Jolas, Eugene, ed. *Anthologie de la Nouvelle Poésie Americaine.* 5th ed. Paris: Kra, 1928.

489. Kerlin, Robert, ed. *Negro Poets and Their Poems.* 3d rev. ed. Washington: Associated Publishers, 1935.

490. Kreymborg, Alfred, ed. *Anthology of American Poetry.* 2d rev. ed. New York: Tudor, 1941.

491. ————. *Lyric America, 1630–1930.* New York: Coward-McCann, 1930.

492. Lieberman, Elias, ed. *Poems for Enjoyment.* New York: Harper & Brothers, 1931.

493. Locke, Alain, ed. *The New Negro.* New York: Boni, 1925.

494. Luccock, Halford E., and Brentano, Frances, eds. *The Questing Spirit: Religion in the Literature of Our Time.* New York: Coward-McCann, 1947.

495. Luciani, Virgilio, ed. *Amore ed Odio di Poeti Negri.* Milan: Casa Editrice Ceschina, 1957.

496. McCullough, Esther Morgan, ed. *As I Pass, O Manhattan.* North Bennington, Vt.: Coley Taylor, 1956.

497. McNeil, Horace J., ed. *Poems for a Machine Age.* New York: McGraw-Hill, 1941.

498. Marcus, Shmuel, ed. *An Anthology of Revolutionary Poetry.* New York: Active Press, 1929.

499. Markham, Edwin, ed. *Book of American Poetry.* New York: William Wise, 1934.

500. *Meine Dunklen Hände: Modern Negerlyrik.* Munich: Nymphenburger Verlagshandlung, 1953.

501. *Los Mejores Versos de la Poesía Negra.* Buenos Aires: Editorial Nuestra America, 1956.

502. Monroe, Harriet, and Henderson, Alice Corbin, eds. *The New Poetry.* New York: Macmillan Co., 1932.

503. Morrison, James Dalton, ed. *Masterpieces of Religious Verse.* New York: Harper & Brothers, 1948.

504. Moult, Thomas, ed. *The Best Poems of 1925.* New York: Harcourt, Brace & Co., 1926.

505. ————. *The Best Poems of 1927.* London: Jonathan Cape, 1927.

506. Pereda Valdes, Ildefonso, ed. *Antologia de la Poesía Negra Americana.* Santiago: Ediciones Ercilla, 1936.

507. Porter, Edna, ed. *Double Blossoms: Helen Keller Anthology.* New York: Lewis Copeland, 1931.

508. Rittenhouse, Jessie, ed. *The Third Book of Modern Verse.* Boston: Houghton Mifflin Co., 1927.

509. Schnittkind, Henry T., ed. *The Poets of the Future: A College Anthology for 1921–1922.* Boston: Stratford Co., 1922.

510. Scollard, Clinton, and Rittenhouse, Jessie B., eds. *Patrician Rhymes.* Boston: Houghton Mifflin Co., 1932.

511. Shipman, Dorothy Middlebrook, ed. *Stardust and Holly: Poems and Songs of Christmas.* New York: Macmillan Co., 1932.

512. Smith, Bernard, ed. *The Democratic Spirit*. New York: Alfred A. Knopf, 1941.

513. Statewide Recreation Project. *The Negro Sings*. Jacksonville, Fla.: n.p., 1940.

514. Strong, Sidney, ed. *We Believe in Immortality: Affirmations by 100 Men and Women*. New York: Coward-McCann, 1929.

515. Thompson, Blanche Jennings, ed. *More Silver Pennies*. New York: Macmillan Co., 1938.

516. U.S. Work Projects Administration, New Jersey. *An Anthology of Negro Poetry by Negroes and Others* [Trenton? 1937].

517. Untermeyer, Louis, ed. *Modern American Poetry*. 5th rev. ed. New York: Harcourt, Brace & Co., 1936.

518. ————. *Modern American Poetry*. 7th rev. ed. New York: Harcourt, Brace & Co., 1950.

519. ————. *The New Modern American and British Poetry*. New York: Harcourt, Brace & Co., 1950.

520. Wagenknecht, Edward, ed. *The Story of Jesus in World Literature*. New York: Creative Age Press, 1946.

521. White, Newman Ivey, and others, eds. *An Anthology of Verse by American Negroes*. Durham, N.C.: Trinity College Press, 1924.

522. Wilkinson, Marguerite, ed. *New Voices*. New York: Macmillan Co., 1928.

523. ————. *Yule Fire*. New York: Macmillan Co., 1925.

# Sources of
# Information

## INDEXES

*Bibliography Index: A Cumulative Bibliography of Bibliographies.* New York: H. W. Wilson Co.

*Biography Index.* New York: H. W. Wilson Co.

*Book Review Digest.* New York: H. W. Wilson Co.

*A Catalog of Books Represented by Library of Congress Printed Cards.* Ann Arbor: J. W. Edwards.

*Cumulative Book Index: World List of Books in the English Language.* New York: H. W. Wilson Co.

*Education Index.* New York: H. W. Wilson Co.

*Essay and General Literature Index.* New York: H. W. Wilson Co.

*International Index to Periodicals.* New York: H. W. Wilson Co.

Leary, Lewis. *Articles on American Literature, 1900–1950.* Durham, N.C.: Duke University Press, 1954.

*New York Times Index.* New York: New York Times Co.
*Readers' Guide to Periodical Literature.* New York: H. W. Wilson Co.
*Union List of Serials in Libraries of the United States and Canada.* New York: H. W. Wilson Co.

## OTHER

Clippings, unpublished papers, and other materials in the possession of Mrs. Ida Mae Cullen, widow of the poet.

Clippings and other material from the following libraries: Schomburg Collection, New York Public Library; Beinecke Rare Books Library, Yale University; The Moorland Room, Howard University.

Hughes, Langston. *The Big Sea*; an autobiography. New York: Hill and Wang, 1963.

Interview with Mrs. Ida Mae Cullen, widow of Countée P. Cullen.

Interviews with Mrs. Jean Blackwell Hutson, Curator, Schomburg Collection, New York Public Library.

Material from issues of *The Magpie*, DeWitt-Clinton High School literary magazine.

*New York Amsterdam News*, 1 April 1950, p. 10.

# Index to
# Titles

---

THE entries in this section are an index to titles in the various collections included in this book. The numbers following the title indicate the entry number in this book's bibliography. The arrangement of titles is alphabetical, word by word.

# INDEX TO TITLES

# Index to Names
# in Chapters 1-3

THIS index covers only Chapters 1 through 3, and the numbers refer to the page that the entry appears on.

*A Bio-Bibliography of Countée P. Cullen, 1903–1946* was composed in Linotype Janson with Janson display type by The Book Press, Brattleboro, Vermont. The entire book was printed by offset lithography.